NOW I CAN SEE

*Some names have been changed for privacy

A Publication of Tall Pine Books

ISBN: 978-1-7353469-8-4

*Printed in the United States of America

NOW I CAN SEE

how *practically* falling in love with
God radically changed my everyday life

Fayth Marie Glock

CONTENTS

DEAR ME   1

1. **ENTERING IN:** REAL STILLNESS   5

2. **THE SECRET PLACE:** REAL LIFE   19

3. **ANYWAYS, ALWAYS:** REAL GRATITUDE   29

4. **I'VE HAD MORE MAGICAL MOMENTS:** REAL ADVENTURE   39

5. **TALK ABOUT RADICAL:** REAL OBEDIENCE   45

6. **SO THIS IS LOVE:** REAL ROMANCE   55

7. **SO THIS IS WHAT IT MEANS:** REAL REST   59

8. **I AM RICH:** REAL WEALTH   63

9. **FOREVER I DO:** REAL LOVE   69

10. **WHY AM I OBSESSED WITH IMPACT?:** REAL PURPOSE   75

11. **STOP ACTING LIKE GROWN UPS:** REAL WONDER   89

12. **LISTENING IS LIFE:** REAL LEADERSHIP   105

13. **WHAT DID YOU DO TODAY?:** REAL PRODUCTIVITY   109

14. **I FEEL IT EVERY DAY:** REAL COMMUNION   115

15. **OWN YOUR BELOVEDNESS:** REAL DELIGHT   127

16. **FOR WHAT?:** REAL ENDURANCE   135

17. **I WILL DANCE WEIRD, NOW:** REAL JOY   143

18. **I WOULDN'T TRADE IT FOR ANYTHING:** REAL FULFILLMENT   149

19. **ALREADY IN LOVE:** REAL CONTENTMENT   153

20. **I HAVE SOMEONE I WANT YOU TO MEET:** REAL TRUST   159

IT WAS THE DAY AFTER CHRISTMAS   177

ACKNOWLEDGMENTS   179

MEET THE AUTHOR   181

ENDNOTES   182

To my Savior, Lover, and Comforter–thank You.

"To love is to be vulnerable."

—*C.S. LEWIS | THE FOUR LOVES*[1]

DEAR ME

THAT MOMENT AS a small child you've always remembered is more significant than you might think.

You sat there on the couch glancing through the half circle-shaped window staring at the bright moon without a blink.

God was speaking to you, delighting in His daughter.

You sat there speechless, mesmerized by your Father.

As you grew, life started to become more complicated.

But God never stopped delighting in you, even though you often forgot to delight in Him, too.

You're so beautiful.

You just don't fully see it yet.

I know you love God so much.

You just haven't yet learned the intimate gaze on you He has set.

Your future is full of pain.

Some of the deepest pain you will ever know.

You will experience loss, hypocrisy, and anguish.

A sadness like a constant, inseparable shadow.

But when you hit the bottom of the pit,

Your face will shift up.

You'll be taught and learn what it means to really *look* and just sit.

I know it doesn't make sense in a worldly context,

But your pain is what will bring you into God-reality.

You'll start to fall in love with the Lord.

And see things you've never seen.

It's not going to be easy.

In fact, your life will often be a lot harder than those around you.

Because you'll learn that a life of *real faith* looks different.

And that God-reality gives you vision to see through.

Right through religion, cultural norms, hypocrisy, and a churched, lukewarm nation.

Jesus, not just as a comforting belief, but an everyday, tangible manifestation.

Your joy, love, freedom, and faith will be a mystery to those around you.

The more you look like Christ, the more the dark in the world will despise you.

But you will learn that nothing else but Christ Himself is your reward.

You'll learn how to practically enter into His presence.

You'll learn that in everything, you can be looking at the Lord.

You'll learn that you, by yourself, are absolutely nothing.

But with God, you are absolutely everything.

He has been speaking to you your whole life.

You will soon learn how to listen.

You have been overthinking your entire life.

But pretty soon even gazing at God's sky will make your eyes glisten.

There is no reason, my child, for any self-criticism or self-condemnation.

Because, dear one, we don't know what we don't know.

And God's timing varies for different lives. Leave to Him the narration.

Because even as I write this, I know in ten years I will probably look back at this and laugh.

Because growing to become more like Jesus is a process, and every mistake we make along the way He has taken upon Himself on our behalf.

Oh, dear one, you are going to see Him *everywhere*.

You'll learn that entering into the secret place is not a moment, but a way of life, a constant prayer.

You may think you know God fully now, but, child, there is so much more to discover.

Oh, my sweet one, you're going to learn that God is not only your Father and friend, but your deep, intimate lover.

For the rest of your life, you'll learn what it really means to live free.

You'll learn to switch from *temporary world* to *eternal real,*

And realize again and again, "*Now I can see.*"

1

ENTERING IN

REAL STILLNESS

I WAS IN an extremely low place.

Spiritually.

Emotionally.

Physically.

Mentally.

I was numb.

In the darkest place I had ever found myself in my young life of twenty-three years at the time.

In a matter of several weeks, my life flipped upside down.

In simple words, everything I thought was… *wasn't*.

Everything I thought was going to happen… *didn't*.

And all of it was taken away from me in a flash, completely out of my control.

I found myself *randomly* at this prayer conference my parents invited me to.

I was on my knees in the sanctuary of a church.

Alone, near the side wall in a walking aisle.

I was trying to "be still."

It wasn't working.

The conference speaker's words struck me:

"You are never truly worshipping God until you forget about yourself."

I was trying to focus on God.

Externally, it may have been quiet.

But internally, the distracting noise blared.

Thoughts, feelings, worries, and pain swam through my heart and brain.

I couldn't seem to turn down my internal noise no matter how hard I tried.

I was trying to worship.

I was trying to hear God.

I was singing and praying, but I felt all over the place.

My frustration flared.

My heart sank.

The speaker's words struck me again:

"Real stillness is the absence of internal noise."

Had I ever been still *for real*?

In my entire life?

Eric Gilmour led the conference.[2]

He was the first person that ever taught me what it *practically* looks like to enter into the presence of God, utilizing a series of simple steps to get ourselves into a place of real stillness.

I was so used to people saying things like *"be still"* and *"rejoice in the Lord"* and *"listen to God."*

But no one really ever *taught me* what those words actually meant in real application, until Eric.

For some reason, I took his teaching and applied it with a deep commitment.

I think I had finally reached such a low and humbled place which enabled me to grasp my insane need for God and dependence on the Holy Spirit.

It didn't look perfect, but I intentionally tried to still myself every day.

Whether I had ten minutes, an hour, or more.

I could be in the car on my way to work or at home on a slow Saturday morning.

I would turn on Eric's instrumental worship music and go through the steps out loud.[3]

As I applied Eric's teaching, my personal steps and rhythm adjusted slightly, mainly in adding a step focused on intentional gratitude.[4]

~

1. POVERTY

Verbally acknowledging my deep need and dependence on the Lord–that I am nothing without Him and completely reliant upon Him. For me, this is also a time of repentance for anything I know I did not glorify the Lord through.

"My God, I am nothing without You! I am fully dependent on You."

> *Blessed [spiritually prosperous, happy, to be admired] are the poor in spirit [those devoid of spiritual arrogance, those who regard themselves as insignificant], for theirs is the Kingdom of heaven [both now and forever].* (Matthew 5:3, AMP)

2. GRATITUDE

Verbally thanking the Lord for who He is and for everything He has provided.

"Oh God, I come with a grateful heart. For everything You are, who I am in You, and all that You have provided for me."

> *Enter his gates with thanksgiving, and his courts with praise!*
> *Give thanks to him; bless his name!* (Psalm 100:4, ESV)

3. STILLNESS

Verbally declaring to the Lord that He has my full and complete attention. This step can take significant time to work through depending on where I am in life. This is where we push through and block out the noise and worries of this world to get to a place of real internal stillness. When I am struggling here, I state specific thoughts I am surrendering: *"I lay down my job... this situation... this person... this pain... this dream..."*

"God, I come to give You my sole focus and complete attention."

4. ADORATION

At this point–after acknowledging that I am nothing without God, thanking Him for who He is and all that I have in Him, and giving Him my sole focus–I am ready to worship Him. This could look different each time and it can be super simple. Sometimes I sing to Him, sometimes I dance, sometimes I simply sit and tell Him what I love about Him. Oftentimes I do nothing but focus on the beauty of the Lord. Some days I might do all or a combination of these.

5. MANIFESTATION

In simple terms, a manifestation is when something becomes real and clear. At this point for me, the steps are done because, during adoration, the Holy Spirit takes over and my heart and mind are ready to receive and listen. Many things could happen. God could give me a certain person to pray for. He might give me a vision, a picture, a Scripture, a specific word. Sometimes I don't really receive anything, and it's simply a time to sit and be with God, free from having an expectation that something certain has to happen. It's a time to linger with the Lord. We don't need to try to make anything happen, we just need to *be*.

The first three steps (poverty, gratitude, and stillness) are what I really needed in order to learn how to *position myself* to hear, see, and listen to God more clearly.

The stillness step was really difficult for me.

I didn't know how to shut my mind off.

How could I stop thinking about work? Relationships? Things I needed to do?

It felt impossible.

Someone at the conference asked Eric for advice on how to do this and one of his tips transformed my relationship with God.

He advised to choose a phrase to keep coming back to.

It could be something like *"Holy holy holy is the Lord God Almighty"* or

"*Great is the Lord and worthy to be praised.*" Anything to get us focused back on the Lord.

He said to repeat the phase every time our minds start to wander.

There were times where it felt like this was all I did…

I tried and tried to forget myself, and would come back to the phrase over and over.

I sometimes felt like a failure.

But then I realized…

How glorifying to God, even if I had to say the phrase fifty times, that I was intentionally striving to be still with Him and give Him my sole focus.

As I practiced, my life began to change.

My circumstances were still the same.

But I was learning to *pay attention* throughout my days.

Intentionally making time to focus on God started to slow my frantic thoughts and worries.

I started seeing and hearing the Holy Spirit more clearly in my everyday moments and tasks.

I was learning to quiet myself so I could hear His voice instead of just my own.

I was training my brain.

I was learning how to resist hurry.

Sitting with Him opened my eyes to what mattered on a daily basis.

Ann Voskamp describes what I was learning well in her devotional, *One Thousand Gifts*:[5]

"Calm. Haste makes waste. Life is not an emergency. Life is brief and it is fleeting, but it is not an emergency... I breathe deep and He preaches to me, soothing the time-frenzied soul with the grace river in whisper. Life is not an emergency."

I was living my daily life as if it were an emergency with constant thoughts, constant tasks, and constant worries.

The hurry was inside of me.

My life continued to be externally busy.

But I learned, as Ann writes, that the fast can have spiritually slow hearts.

~

Eric explained that *"diligence will become delight."*

As human beings, if we want something to become natural and enjoyable, we have to commit ourselves to practicing it.

Such as playing the piano or juggling a soccer ball.

It might be frustrating in the beginning, but later it becomes enjoyable.

I used to be afraid when I was reading the Bible or spending time with God that I was just doing it as a "to-do" list item.

This resulted in me just not doing it, because I didn't want my motivation to be off.

But the thing is, we have to start somewhere.

We must commit to a rhythm in order for it to become a joy and something we *want* to do.

Just like music or a sport, it takes intentionality for it to become natural.

And this takes time.

The amount of time it takes will look different for different people.

We cannot try it a couple times, become discouraged, and give up.

We have to make a choice to condition ourselves to be still.

> Intimacy grows deeper and God's voice becomes clearer-with intentional time.

Intimacy grows deeper and God's voice becomes clearer—with intentional time.

As humans, it's easy for us to be quick to say that we don't have time, but the reality is, we do have time.

It's not a time issue.

It's a priority issue.

God was way nearer than I realized.

I just hadn't learned what it meant to create space to hear Him.

I had known a lot about God before and genuinely loved Him.

I understood that reading God's Word and prayer were extremely important in daily life.

I knew the power of the Holy Spirit.

But I was going a thousand miles per hour.

I learned that sitting still in the presence of God is the single most important thing in my daily life.

Like Jesus modeled for me, I must get away from society and simply be with my Father.

I may have known a lot *about Him*, but I didn't fully *know Him*.

I learned that there is so much more.

I started receiving visions, dreams, and encouraging prophetic words for others.

In time, I learned that what I thought was supernatural was actually extremely natural.

> I learned that sitting still in the presence of God is the single most important thing in my daily life.
>
> Like Jesus modeled for me, I must get away from society and simply be with my Father.

Stilling myself also allowed me to read the Word of God with a focus I didn't know possible, experiencing God like I never had before through the Scriptures.

Pretty soon my daily "balanced diet of Scripture" (as Eric put it) changed from an "I should" into a genuine "I want to."

More than all of that though, daily entering into God's presence is what brought me into a real, loving, tangible, consistent relationship with God.

I learned what Jesus meant when He told His disciples that it was better if He left, because once He did, He would send the Helper, the Holy Spirit, to us (John 16:7).

Jesus in the flesh couldn't be with every single person at every moment.

The Holy Spirit is tangibly present with us, everywhere and always.

I could have given up that day, kneeling on the church floor in frustrating heartache.

But instead, thankfully, I poured out my sadness and anger before God.

I lamented forward.

I cried and was just honest with Him.

Anyone can apply these steps.

But they are only effective if we apply them with our whole heart.

In total, transparent surrender.

NOW I can see.

The Lord is near to the brokenhearted and saves the crushed in spirit. (Psalm 34:18, ESV)

The Lord will fight for you; you need only to be still. (Exodus 14:14, NIV)

"It takes time for our eyes to adjust to stillness, and only the slow really see."

—ANN VOSKAMP | ONE THOUSAND GIFTS[6]

2

THE SECRET PLACE

REAL LIFE

AT THE CONFERENCE, God gave me a vision that was vividly clear, an experience I hadn't ever really had before, at least not that clear.

It was me in a stunning meadow.

Nothing I could express accurately with words.

Mountains surrounded a valley with an extraordinary, vast meadow.

The sound of rushing water was somewhere nearby.

Vibrant colors were everywhere I looked—a piercing blue sky, greener than green grass, and multi-colored flowers speckled across the meadow.

It was the softest grass I had ever felt, a softness I couldn't begin to imagine on earth.

I wore an ivory cotton dress.

Buttons on the front, a flowing skirt that hit mid calf, a high neckline, short sleeves, and a beautiful yet simple embroidery pattern across the whole dress.

So comfortable and free.

My soft brown hair cascaded down my back, natural and stunning with gentle waves.

My eyes glowed emerald.

It was me, but it was unlike any face I'd ever seen.

I realized my face probably looked different because there was no sin... no hardship... no evil.

And with no sin, I imagine this would change everything about our eyes and facial expressions.

I was with God. I can't fully explain what He looked like.

But He was vast, extremely comforting, and present with me.

We were spending time together.

I propped my head up on His lap like a child would.

I gazed at Him and listened to Him talk.

I blabbed a bunch to Him and He chuckled.

He patted me off like a child into the meadow and I ran around, danced, and sang.

It then came time to leave.

I walked up to God and He gave me five large seeds.

He told me exactly where to place them.

I went back out into the world, still in my ivory dress.

I saw myself in everyday places.

My office, my church, the grocery, my neighborhood.

Dancing my way through the streets and buildings, placing the seeds in super specific spots.

I can remember that I placed one seed on a particular person's desk at work.

Exactly where God told me to put it.

When I finished, I went back to my "secret place" meadow to be with God again.

This pattern repeated.

I would spend time with God, go back out into the world with my seeds, and then go back to Him.

When thinking about this vision, a piercing question came to me:

What if I never went back?

I imagined myself placing the seeds and then, instead of going back to God, taking matters into my own hands and going to the store to buy a big bag of seeds.

I would then take these purchased seeds and place them everywhere with no rhyme or reason, thinking I was doing good things and helping people.

And pretty soon I would become exhausted… worn out… discouraged.

Because these store-bought seeds wouldn't work.

Because I hadn't gotten them from the right source.

Because I didn't get them from God.

I will tell people this vision until the day I die.

Because it vividly explains what it means to live real life effectively on earth.

It is this balance of intentionally being with God, and then going out into the world in His name.

We are weak, broken people.

We can't survive sustainably outside of the secret place for very long.

We have to go back.

Our effectiveness as believers can only come from a place of real intimacy with God.

When we try to do it on our own, we become exhausted and fail.

I imagine a dad making cookies with his three-year-old, the child watching him with bright eyes.

It would be much faster for the parent to just make the cookies and be done with it.

But he knows that it will bring the child joy to be a part of the process.

So he allows the child to pour in the chocolate chips and mix the batter, making a complete mess while doing so.

Isn't it this way with us and God?

He doesn't need us to do anything.

In fact, it would be a lot easier for Him to just take care of everything Himself.

But God gives us the joy in partnering with Him, regardless of the mess we might make in the process.

Doing things for and with God is never a burden or a pressure.

But instead, an incredible gift and honor.

I can remember clearly one day at work when I was extremely frustrated.

My shoulders felt heavy and I was stressed out of my mind.

A thought suddenly hit me.

I need to go back.

I realized that I had drifted from Him and this was why I didn't feel at peace.

I had gone too long without going to my secret place.

I was looking at the world too much and not at Him.

I had gone too many hours without making His presence my priority.

Since receiving this vision about myself, I have had the same exact vision for countless others.

With the same scenery and clothing.

I've had the same vision for men as well, wearing a long white shirt and pants instead of a dress.

At first, I questioned myself.

Am I just thinking the same vision over and over?

But then I realized, I wasn't.

God was just giving me pictures of what life can look like for any of His children.

A life lived in love with God.

A life lived in peace and wonder, not because of circumstance, but because of His presence.

A life lived out of the secret place.

NOW I can see.

> *He that dwelleth in the secret place of the most High shall abide under the shadow of the Almighty.* (Psalm 91:1, KJV)

THE REST OF THIS BOOK is a series of simple stories and moments, in no particular order, that led me to see and experience God-reality more clearly. These stories contain real joy, pain, dreams, sorrow–real life. Like many of you, I am fighting against darkness and what my world and culture says I should and shouldn't do. And instead, doing my best to live according to God's Word and voice alone. As I continue to fall in love with God, heaven becomes more real and this earthly life starts to fade away.

So join me.

Out of the lukewarm and into the real.

May we persevere to the end.

As Steffany Gretzinger sings in her song "All That Lives Forever,"

"Death is just a door to lead us home to You."[7]

> ***Steep yourself*** *in God-reality, God-initiative, God-provisions.* (Luke 12:31, MSG, emphasis added)

> *But the one who **endures** to the end will be saved.* (Matthew 24:13, ESV, emphasis added)

> *For to me, living means living for Christ, and dying is even **better**.* (Philippians 1:21, NLT, emphasis added)

> ***Be prepared***. *You're up against far more than you can handle on your own. Take all the help you can get, every weapon God has issued, so that when it's all over but the shouting **you'll still be on your feet. Truth, righteousness, peace, faith, and salvation are more than words. Learn how to apply them.** You'll need them throughout your life. God's Word is an indispensable weapon. In the*

same way, prayer is essential in this ongoing warfare. Pray hard and long. Pray for your brothers and sisters. Keep your eyes open. Keep each other's spirits up so that no one falls behind or drops out. And don't forget to pray for me. **Pray that I'll know what to say and have the courage to say it at the right time, telling the mystery to one and all,** *the Message that I, jailbird preacher that I am, am responsible for getting out.* (Ephesians 6:13-20, MSG, emphasis added)

3

ANYWAYS, ALWAYS

REAL GRATITUDE

I GREW UP going to a lake in Michigan in the summers.

It's where my parents met and fell in love. Their families both had a cottage on either side of the lake and still do to this day.

Late summer nights, slow mornings, and countless hours of swimming with cousins fills my childhood memories.

Our cottage has always been full with my parents, siblings, grandparents, aunt and uncle, and cousins—all under one roof.

As far back as I can remember, my grandparents and I have shared a room at the cottage.

I've always loved it.

Next to their queen bed sits my twin daybed.

I have many memories of late night chats with my grandma, whispering in the dark as our faces were only separated by a few feet.

Sometimes my grandpa would throw pillows across the room at me in the dead of the night, often resulting in a back and forth war until my grandma woke up.

Otherwise, he just snored extremely loud.

To the point of waking himself up with one of his aggressive, pig-like snorts.

I always knew I would have a permanent bed in our small cottage regardless of how big the family grew–because no one wanted to sleep in the same room as my grandpa, HA.

Thankfully I am a heavy sleeper and it's never bothered me.

After several decades, my grandparents randomly switched sides of the bed.

I now wake up next to my grandpa.

———

It was about 8:00 AM on a familiar Saturday morning.

I had a long, tiring week at work.

I woke up and was happy to be reminded that I was at the lake and not at home–this meant rest.

My grandpa was up, too.

We made eye contact and exchanged sleepy smiles.

He put his hand out. I offered mine in return.

There we were, holding hands across the small gap between our beds.

Both shutting our eyes, enjoying a few more minutes of sleep.

I recognized the sacredness of the moment.

I knew these moments wouldn't last forever.

In another decade, my grandparents would probably not be with me on earth anymore.

When he let go, I hopped out of my bed, went to the end of their bed, and slid up the middle.

I hugged my grandma awake, saying good morning in a weird, silly voice.

My grandpa chuckled.

These are the moments.

Moments worth holding sacred.

Moments to breath in gratitude, and breathe out praise.

I was twenty-five in that moment.

It probably sounds like I was ten.

I recognize the lies I could have believed.

You are behind... you should be in bed with a husband, not your grandparents... you are lame...

Satan often tempts me to feel ungrateful, jealous, stupid, incomplete.

That I should be longing for a husband above all.

But I know Satan will try to tempt me no matter what I have or don't have.

I cannot fall into my culture's temptation of waiting for certain cultural milestones.

To fall into living in discontentment.

That morning, I was thankfully caught up in the awe, the light, the gift.

If I were married that morning, I wouldn't have gotten to hold my grandpa's hand across the gap.

This small but significant moment reminds me how quickly we can fall into complaining instead of beholding.

I realize now that learning gratitude has played a huge role in my relationship with the Lord because it has taught me how to notice.

I love Ann Voskamp's writing.

She teaches practical gratitude.

She dares us to intentionally notice the ways God loves us wherever we are.

She encourages a life where we literally write down the ways that God loves us every day, a practice I do every morning now before work.

She wrote in a post on her Facebook page,

"...And it's true: brilliant people don't deny the dark; they are the ones who never stop looking for the light in everything."[8]

I so agree–to me, the wisest and most joyful people are the ones who acknowledge the dark, yet never stop looking for the light.

One of my dearest friends, Anna, gave me Ann Voskamp's devotional, *One Thousand Gifts*, when I was in college.[9]

I have read through it four times and counting.

Many of her quotes have impacted my life:

*"A sacrifice of thanks lays down our perspective and raises hands in praise **anyways—always**."*

This small but significant moment reminds me how quickly we can fall into complaining instead of beholding.

"The life that counts blessings discovers its yielding more than it seems."

"In naming that which is right before me, that which I'd otherwise miss, the invisible becomes visible."

*"Instead of filling with expectations, **the joy-filled expect nothing—and are***

filled. *This breath! This oak tree! This daisy! This work! This sky! These people! This place! This day! Surprise!"*

"Count one thousand gifts, bless the Holy One one hundred times a day, commune with His presence filling the laundry room, the kitchen, the hospital, the graveyard, the highways and byways and workways and all the blazing starways, His presence filling me. This is what it means to fully live."

"Before I knew it, thankfulness to God began to fully change me."

Like Ann, gratitude is transforming who I am.

I realize the glory and awe is always there.

Always *here*.

I must be disciplined enough *to see*.

To pause.

To thank.

To praise.

As we do this, our lives can be transformed from dissatisfaction to everyday wonder.

We were created to look at God in all things.

And thank Him in all things.

My favorite book is *The Hiding Place* by Corrie ten Boom.[10]

She and her family were Christians in Amsterdam during the Holocaust and saved hundreds of Jews, eventually being arrested and placed in a concentration camp.

One of my favorite stories of gratitude comes from a moment between Corrie and her sister Betsie, right in the middle of one of the darkest periods in history.

They were placed in a different living barrack.

A barrack designed to house four hundred people was housing fourteen hundred prisoners.

A filthy building missing half its windows.

Bunks piled three high, infested with fleas, and reeking with already slept upon straw from other suffering prisoners.

Betsie believed the answer to the fleas and their terrible living condition was to thank God.

She brought up 1 Thessalonians 5:16-18:

> *Rejoice always, pray continually, give thanks in all circumstances; for this is God's will for you in Christ Jesus.* (NIV)

She told Corrie that they could start by thanking God for everything about their new barracks.

She thanked God that she and her sister were together, that they were miraculously able to sneak a Bible in, and that they had the privilege of sharing the Word of God with the other women.

She even thanked God for the fleas.

Corrie pushed back on this, but Betsie responded saying that they were to give thanks in *all circumstances*, not just in pleasant ones.

Betsie and Corrie started holding services to share the Gospel with the other women.

The risk in getting caught was a sure death.

But night after night, no guard came near and they were even able to hold a secondary service.

They later found out that the reason guards were not coming near was because of the flea infestation.

Corrie wrote,

"My mind rushed back to our first hour in this place. I remembered Betsie's bowed head, remembered her thanks to God for creatures I could see no use for."

If Betsie can thank God for fleas in the middle of a real-life horror story, I can thank God for literally everything in my life.

I had two choices that morning in my daybed.

To complain, or behold.

Thanksgiving is a sacrifice.

An everyday discipline.

If Betsie can thank God for fleas in the middle of a real-life horror story, I can thank God for literally everything in my life.

But discipline becomes delight as giving thanks becomes our default.

We are able to have eyes filled with God-wonder in good times and bad when we see the world through the lens of God's goodness.

When we have Him, we are not in want, and have everything in the reality of His presence.

No matter what comes in this life,

May I lay down my perspective.

And raise my hands in praise.

Anyways, *always.*

NOW I can see.

> *When the time came, Jesus and the apostles sat down together at the table. Jesus said, "I have been very eager to eat this Passover meal with you before my suffering begins. For I tell you now that I won't eat this meal again until its meaning is fulfilled in the Kingdom of God." Then he took a cup of wine and* **gave thanks** *to God for it. Then he said, "Take this and share it among yourselves. For I will not drink wine again until the Kingdom of God has come." He took some bread and* **gave thanks** *to God for it. Then he broke it in pieces and gave it to the disciples, saying, "This is my body, which is given for you. Do this in remembrance of me." After supper he took another cup of wine and said, "This cup is the new covenant between God and his people—an agreement confirmed with my blood, which is poured out as a sacrifice for you." (Luke 22:14-20, NLT, emphasis added)*

4

I'VE HAD MORE MAGICAL MOMENTS

REAL ADVENTURE

I WAS STANDING on a mountaintop in Nepal, a small country sandwiched between China and India.

I was gazing at the scenery below me.

It felt fake—it was so stunning.

The white-capped Himalayas, the what-seemed-to-be tiny town far below, the glistening lake.

This was one of those "picture-perfect" moments.

A thought popped in my head:

I've had more magical moments in my living room in Indiana.

I hate when Christians feel some sort of weird shame or inferiority if they have never been out of the country or on any sort of "missions trip."

I treasure my times abroad, but the deep truth hit me in that moment that it just doesn't matter where we are, *ever*.

For real though.

My everyday, alone moments with God mean way more than any sort of exotic experience I've ever had.

I encounter Him just as powerfully or even more so on my daily drives, at my kitchen table, or dancing in my living room.

When I learned how to still myself and started to experience God in ways I didn't know existed, I was living alone.

I can remember making that decision.

I had always had roommates, and I am pretty social and outgoing.

I wavered back and forth in my mind, but I knew in my spirit that my next step was to live alone.

I didn't really know why, and many people told me it was not the right decision.

That I would be lonely, sad, etc.

But I knew God's voice was more important than any voices around me.

With faith and about 70% certainty, I moved into a new place alone.

I realize now that God needed to get me alone so He could wake me up to His wonder.

He needed to teach me how to commune with Him outside of the influence of other people.

He taught me to go to Him first, rather than going to a human before going to Him.

I realized that He is ultimately my main source of intimacy, community, rest, and adventure.

—

I started thinking a lot about the current state of the American Church during my time living alone.

When I learned and experienced what it really means to praise God, I understood that church is supposed to be an *extension* of our worship.

An extension of our worship from our everyday lives.

I realized that the most important, most enjoyable, most sacred times of worship in life are the ones that are often unseen and simple.

Laying alone in bed at night whispering with God.

Worshiping Him in the car.

> I realized that He is ultimately my main source of intimacy, community, rest, and adventure.

On my knees in the middle of my living room alone, singing my heart out to Him.

In my cubicle during my first adult job, swaying to my music with eyes closed for a sacred moment.

If I am not worshiping the Lord when I am alone during the week, is the raising of my hands at a church only on Sunday mornings even fully real?

If I am not living in awe in my everyday moments, is the temporary awe on a mountaintop even that meaningful?

I can remember another thought I had on that mountaintop in Nepal.

I miss God.

He was with me, of course.

But I was co-leading a trip and every day was exhausting and full.

I realized how badly I was aching to sit alone with God, because I was out of my normal routine with Him and I was with people all the time.

I loved the trip, but I was genuinely excited to get back to my everyday moments with God.

I started to understand Jesus more and what He modeled for us in His life on earth.

> If I am not living in awe in my everyday moments, is the temporary awe on a mountaintop even that meaningful?

He left His disciples and the crowds that followed Him all of the time to be alone with God.

He slipped away to be with His Father not only to seek wisdom, but because He loved His Father and wanted to be with Him.

Every genuine moment I have with God, the literal Creator of the galaxies, is more magical than anything I could ever imagine.

Anywhere can be my sanctuary.

NOW I can see.

> *While it was still night, way before dawn, he got up and went out to a secluded spot and prayed.* (Mark 1:35, MSG)
>
> *At about that same time he climbed a mountain to pray. He was there all night in prayer before God.* (Luke 6:12, MSG)
>
> *With the crowd dispersed, he climbed the mountain so he could be by himself and pray. He stayed there alone, late into the night.* (Matthew 14:23, MSG)

5

TALK ABOUT RADICAL

REAL OBEDIENCE

I WAS CATCHING up with one of my most beloved friends, Savannah.

We didn't see each other as much as we wanted to, but always deeply cherished any time we did spend together.

We were sitting in my living room exchanging life updates.

I am so *for* Savannah and she is so *for* me.

All we do (besides laughing and being crazy weirdos) is encourage each other to look at God.

To continue.

To keep being faithful.

I told her my updates about work and working remotely because of the coronavirus pandemic.

Sav talked about her first year of marriage and what it had been like to navigate life with a spouse, as well as updates on her job as a leader in youth ministry.

I loved hearing her passionately and wholeheartedly share stories about students coming to the Lord, summer camp, missions trips, life with her husband—all of it.

I couldn't help but notice the contrast of our lives.

At that point, at the same age, obedience to God looked very different for us.

Right then, obedience for Sav was to pour her heart into youth ministry, coach junior high volleyball, and love her husband.

Right then, obedience for me was to work remotely ten hours a day alone and write a book.

I couldn't help but think of the components of her life I desired.

At the end of our conversation, I brought up the contrast and I said something that I knew would stick with me possibly forever.

"Obedience to God cannot be compared. Obedience looks different for every life."

Oftentimes, it seems our Christian culture does not support this truth at all.

It seems to glamorize certain jobs and certain missions.

From my perspective, this sometimes tends to create a divide between sacred and secular.

> Obedience to God cannot be compared. Obedience looks different for every life.

I can remember struggling so much when I knew God was calling me to a corporate job and to get my master's in business following my undergrad.

I didn't want to at all.

But even though I didn't want to, I felt so much peace and joy when I accepted the job simply because I knew I was yielding to God and listening to Him.

I can vividly remember a painful moment my senior year of college.

A girl in my major asked me what I was going to do after graduation.

I told her and then politely asked what her plans were.

She said something along the lines of,

"Oh, I decided to not go that route. I feel called to ministry."

If she only knew that my aching heart's one desire was to pursue God with everything I was...

And that is exactly what I was doing.

But to her, I had chosen something that wasn't "ministry."

For me personally, it would have been a lot easier, and way more natural, to travel abroad and serve as a "missionary" right after college.

How much easier for me it would have been to join a so-called "ministry" rather than entering the corporate world.

It seems to be a stereotype that going abroad is the "biggest, godliest sacrifice."

For me, this would have been a lot easier than going into a business setting.

Obedience does not always look like we think it should.

I wanted other Christians to look at my life and affirm that I was "doing the Lord's work."

A traditional "missionary" is visible.

Everyone knows they are dedicating their life to serving God.

People see the newsletters… the fundraising campaigns… the "here I am send me" social media post…

For me, on the other hand, I just looked… normal.

The real issue was that I cared.

I cared about my image.

I was making one of the biggest sacrifices of my life and no one really acknowledged it.

Because I was pursuing a "normal, American choice."

Sacrifice looks completely different than I thought.

And it doesn't matter if other people can physically see the sacrifice or not.

Sacrifice looks completely different for different lives.

In my experience, the word *ministry* has been abused.

To the point where I sometimes avoid using the word.

Every follower of Jesus who is legitimately committed to Him is a minister.

Every day, everywhere.

Every smile.

Every daily transaction.

Every conversation.

Every job.

Out of our intimacy with God, we listen to Him and do what He shows us to do.

That is an obedient life.

If He tells me to travel to Asia to love His people there, I must go.

If He tells me to work at a bank and love His people there, I must go.

If He tells me to take a year off and spend time with | Sacrifice looks completely different for different lives.

Him alone to prepare for something in the future, I must do it.

Obedience does not always look like obedience to other humans.

God calls us to do different things at different times.

And only His voice and opinion matters.

I hear many Christians say things along the lines of *"God will never take you somewhere you're not supposed to be."*

I agree, but only if the individual is actually yielding to God.

If we are not spending time with God and listening to Him, how would we ever know where we are supposed to go and what we are supposed to do?

It seems to me that people sometimes use phrases like this to justify poor decisions.

Decisions made without asking God about it first.

We cannot let culture define what a radical life for God looks like.

Early on at my first job out of college, an awesome, older Christian woman in my department asked me to get coffee.

I now realize she could easily see that I was on the struggle bus, HA.

I started babbling to her about how frustrated I was and how I so badly wanted to live a "radical life" for God.

Her response is something that altered my view of obedience entirely.

"Radical, huh? How about a young woman who sought God for direction and heard God tell her to go into the corporate world and to get her MBA and even though she didn't want to do it at all, she did it anyway. Talk about radical."

It still blows my perspective every time I think about it.

I was already living a radical life and I didn't even know it.

I had just let my culture define what a radical life meant, instead of letting God define my unique, radical life.

In God-reality, a radical life is being obedient to God, period.

⁓

When we become obsessed with being "radical for God" in an unhealthy way, I call this "the purpose grip."

Our fists become clenched so tight because we become obsessed with trying to figure out what our purpose is.

I had just let my culture define what a radical life meant, instead of letting God define my unique, radical life.

We must understand that our purpose has already been defined.

When we realize that our purpose has already been defined, we no longer have to live a life striving to define our purpose.

When our fists are clenched so tight, it's much harder to notice what's right in front of us.

When we understand that we were designed to have an intimate relationship with God and simply partner with Him in life out of that place of love, our clenched fists can start to loosen.

And we can start to actually see.

That we are free.

That the pressure is off.

That the world around us is beautiful.

That His presence is our purpose.

And that following God's voice is never a burden, but an honor.

One of the most powerful things I have ever heard God say to me was,

"Satan is threatened by your obedience."

When we realize that our purpose has already been defined, we no longer have to live a life striving to define our purpose.

I will continue living in my unique, radical obedience as defined by God until the day I die.

When I was sitting on that couch listening to Savannah talk about her life, I was tempted to be jealous.

But since I know what obedience really means, I can encourage everyone around me to live out their obedience–with joy and confidence, instead of comparison.

And ultimately?

I am obedient because I love God.

NOW I can see.

> *The person who has My commandments and keeps them is the one who [really] loves Me; and whoever [really] loves Me will be loved by My Father, and I will love him and reveal Myself to him [I will make Myself real to him].* (John 14:21, AMP)

6

SO THIS IS LOVE

REAL ROMANCE

I WAS WORKING from home alone during the coronavirus pandemic.

I was designing a website for a utility vehicle company and felt overwhelmed with my workload.

My worship music playlist was on.

I was super focused and not paying attention to the music, until a certain song caught my attention.

A song I would usually skip whenever it came on.

He had sung this to me.

The man I thought I loved, trusted, and looked up to spiritually.

The one who suddenly turned the other way and chose to lie to me, neglect me, and dishonor me.

Leaving me in a great state of spiritual confusion, loss, and the darkest hurt I had ever known.

I remember him texting me a video of him singing the song, with a message something along the lines of,

"I was singing this song and I couldn't stop thinking of how beautiful you are."

The hurt and the betrayal could still make my eyes water when I thought about it, even though a significant amount of time had passed.

For some reason, I let the song keep playing.

I realized in that moment how far I had come.

I knew my worth.

My beauty.

My character.

My strength.

Only because, by the grace of God, the Holy Spirit comforted me and spoke to me in my darkness, reminding me continuously of who I really was: a daughter of the King worthy to be cherished and honored.

I listened to the words in the song as Steffany Gretzinger sang, hearing the words straight from the heart of Jesus.[11]

'Cause I loved you before you knew it was love
And I saw it all, still I chose the cross
*And **you were the one that I was thinking of***
When I rose from the grave
Now rid of the shackles, My victory's yours
*I tore the veil **for you to come close***
There's no reason to stand at a distance anymore
You're not far from home

And now I'll be your lighthouse
When you're lost at sea
And I will illuminate everything
No need to be frightened by intimacy
No, just throw off your fear
And come running to Me

The words hit some place in my heart I didn't know existed.

Painful yet joyful tears came to my eyes.

I then saw myself in my mind's eye, in my secret place meadow with God.

There I was in glowing ivory.

Dancing, spinning, and delighting in His presence.

My head reeled back in wondrous, free, contented laughter as I spun around to look at Him.

And then I heard God speak to me, right there at my desk.

"Let this be My love song to you."

My heart felt wrung and refreshed at the same time as confusing pain and God's piercing love mixed together.

I sat there still looking at the same screen of utility vehicles, my hand paused on the mouse.

The words in the song were really true.

I really was the one He was thinking of.

God *sees me*.

And I *see Him*.

I glanced out my window into the gray day, eyes watering.

So this is love.

NOW I can see.

> *So we have come to know and to believe the love that God has for us. God is love, and whoever abides in love abides in God, and God abides in him.* (1 John 4:16, ESV)

7

SO THIS IS WHAT IT MEANS

REAL REST

IT WAS THE next day after listening to Steffany Gretzinger's song, "Out of Hiding," and hearing God speak to me about it being His love song to me.[12]

It was another normal work day from home.

I was still overwhelmed.

Still by myself.

As I worked, the song came to mind again.

I located the song and played it *on purpose.*

I paused my work and sang the lyrics out loud.

A few lines stood out:

*You've got your reasons, **but I hold your peace***...
And I saw it all, still I chose the cross...
You were the one I was thinking of *when I rose from the grave...*
*I tore the veil **for you to come close**...*

I lingered for a moment.

I felt... rested.

Even though I had many reasons to feel stressed.

So this is what it means.

This is what it means in Matthew 11:30 when Jesus says,

> *For my yoke is easy and my burden is light.* (ESV)

I looked up the passage on my computer in The Message version. I loved how verses 28-30 read:

> *Are you tired? Worn out? Burned out on religion? Come to me.* ***Get away with me and you'll recover your life.*** *I'll show you how to take a **real rest**. Walk with me and work with me—watch how I do it. **Learn the unforced rhythms of grace**. I won't lay anything heavy or ill-fitting on you. **Keep company with me** and you'll learn to live **freely** and **lightly**.* (emphasis added)

So that's it then.

Real rest has nothing to do with my circumstances.

His presence is what makes me feel light.

Whether I'm thriving or just barely surviving, it doesn't matter.

The reason He tore the veil was so I could come close to Him.

So that I could nestle my head into His chest.

Jesus didn't come so that I could just read about Him… know facts about Him… attend services about Him… listen to other people talk about Him…

He came so I could personally *experience* Him.

> Real rest has nothing to do with my circumstances. His presence is what makes me feel light.

Hear Him… talk to Him… delight in Him… sing with Him… relax with Him… know Him.

And rest in His reality.

As the work tasks and frustrating messages kept pouring in, I felt calm and chill.

Only because of *Him*.

NOW I can see.

8

I AM RICH

REAL WEALTH

AFTER CHURCH ON a winter Sunday, I went to the grocery to grab a few items for the week.

I had a short list in one hand and my grocery bag in the other.

I walked inside and, in the first aisle, the salsa I usually buy caught my eye.

It wasn't on my list because I had an almost full jar in my fridge.

But I figured I might as well buy another jar for when it ran out.

I reached out to grab the salsa that was at my eye level.

My hand paused as a thought struck me:

The fact that I can buy this unnecessary salsa without a second thought... I am one of the richest people in the world.

I felt the warmth of God's presence then.

I had every reason to dance through the rest of the aisles.

But instead, I walked like a normal human and placed the items I needed in my bag.

Of course, I ended up getting more items I thought of, and pretty soon, I was that awkward person who should have gotten a cart, waddling around with a bag way too full that could burst at any second.

I checked out with my items and waddled once again to my car.

My car started up right away as it always did–*I am rich.*

I plugged my phone in and placed it on the dash mount–*I am rich.*

I drove out of the parking lot to drive home–*I am rich.*

A reminder popped up on my phone:

The joy of the Lord is your strength. (Nehemiah 8:10, ESV)

I. Am. Rich!

As I was driving, a vivid memory flashed in my mind from a couple years prior.

I was working at my first job out of college and adulting for the first time.

A coworker invited me to attend her church because I didn't know where I was going to go yet as I hadn't lived in the city for very long.

I felt awkward walking in by myself. I wasn't used to that.

I felt weird leaving alone, too.

After saying goodbye to my coworker and her family, I went to my car.

I sat there feeling more alone than I had ever felt.

What do I do now?

It was one of my first weekends not in college or living with my family.

I sat there with a blank stare.

I didn't notice that my car started.

I didn't notice that I had a phone.

I didn't notice that I could go get whatever food I wanted.

Instead, I noticed everything I didn't have and wanted in that moment and cried.

⁓

From a worldly standpoint, these two scenarios were a very similar day.

A Sunday where I went to church alone and left church alone.

Yet everything in my heart, mind, and spirit were different.

From crying alone in my car, to being alone in a grocery store giddy over the fact that I had the privilege of being able to buy salsa.

On either day, I had a choice.

⁓

Being able to buy unnecessary salsa places me extremely high on the economic scale in terms of global wealth percentages.

The amount I spent on that salsa, for some people, could be more than what they have to live on for an entire day.

But I realize, this is not what actually makes me rich.

We could have every material thing in the world, but still be the one sobbing in the car.

We could be surrounded by hundreds of people who genuinely love us, and still feel completely alone.

I am rich because the joy of the Lord is my strength–*for real.*

I am rich, because I have learned that feeling lonely has nothing to do with not being surrounded by people, and everything to do with *not realizing* that I am tangibly surrounded by God.

I know that His presence is my wealth.

Because in His presence is where I've actually found consistent, real contentment.

I am rich, because I have learned that feeling lonely has nothing to do with not being surrounded by people, and everything to do with not realizing that I am tangibly surrounded by God.

Consistent, real joy.

Even over a simple jar of salsa.

NOW I can see.

> *Don't hoard treasure down here where it gets eaten by moths and corroded by rust or—worse!—stolen by burglars. Stockpile treasure in heaven, where it's safe from moth and rust and burglars. It's obvious, isn't it? The place where your treasure is, is the place you will most want to be, and end up being.* (Matthew 6:19-21, MSG)

9

FOREVER I DO

REAL LOVE

I WAS LISTENING to my "Sweet Love" music playlist.

"I Get to Love You" by Ruelle came on.[13]

I love the song.

But it hurt too much.

Any love song was all too relatable.

All too painful.

I would have to skip it.

But then, a simple shift happened, one that would change the way I listen to love songs for forever hopefully.

I all of a sudden heard the words not in application to a romantic, human relationship, but instead heard the words from God to me and me to God.

One look at you, my whole life falls in line
I prayed for you before I called you mine

Oh, I can't believe it's true sometimes
Oh, I can't believe it's true

I get to love you
It's the best thing that I'll ever do
I get to love you
It's a promise I'm making to you

Whatever may come, your heart, I will choose
Forever I'm yours, forever I do
I get to love you, I get to love you

The way you love, it changes who I am
I am undone, and I thank God once again...

In my mind's eye, I saw myself in my secret place once again.

Dancing with God.

I could see the glow in my eyes and the loving radiance in His.

There could be no truer words.

One look at Him, and my whole life falls in line.

The way He loves me completely changes who I am.

A few thankful tears made their way down my face.

From that day on, love song after love song after love song reminded me of me and God.

"I Can't Help Falling in Love with You" (Elvis Presley)[14]

Take my hand,
Take my whole life, too
For I can't help falling in love with you...

"When I'm With You" (Ben Rector)[15]

But when I'm with you I'm no longer wandering
And when I'm with you, I swear I can breathe
When I'm with you, I know who I am and who I want to be...

"Run to You" (Lea Michele)[16]

You're beautiful when you look at me
Let's give love another life
Cause you'll be safe in these arms of mine
Just call my name on the edge of the night
And I'll run to you...

"This I Promise you" (*NSYNC)[17] (let's go 90s kids, HA)

When the visions around you
Bring tears to your eyes
And all that surrounds you
Are secrets and lies
I'll be your strength

I'll give you hope
Keeping your faith when it's gone
The one you should call
Was standing there all along
And I will take you in my arms
And hold you right where you belong
'Til the day my life is through
This I promise you
This I promise you

I looked up why Ruelle wrote "I Get to Love You."[18]

She had painfully walked away from a three-and-a-half year long relationship, believing it was the right thing to do.

She had been convinced he was the one she was going to marry.

Six months after the breakup, the man she did marry entered her life.

She wrote the song for their first dance at their wedding.

In her explanation she wrote,

"Sometimes our greatest disappointments in life lead to our greatest gain."

I felt this.

I look back now at some of my darkest moments and losses and realize God was protecting me.

I realize His plans are greater and that the pain I experienced was worth it.

Physical touch has always been important to me in terms of love language.

I've always desired to be held and cherished by a man.

I still do.

One day while I was working, God gave me a vision that hit a deep place in my heart that He and only He knew existed.

In my mind's eye—the eyes of my heart—I saw me and God in our secret place.

We were dancing and He stopped and looked into my eyes intently.

He gently placed His large hand behind my neck, slowly pulled me close to Him, and tenderly kissed me on the forehead.

God knew this was something simple I had always wanted.

Something I had never experienced.

I cried.

I was wrong.

This type of touch was something I had already experienced after all.

Human love, no matter how healthy, will always disappoint in some way at one stage or another.

God's everlasting, unconditional love replaces and heals all pain.

And fulfills all dreams.

So I will always sing,

"Forever I do."

NOW I can see.

> *The Lord your God is in your midst,*
> *a mighty one who will save;*
> *he will rejoice over you with gladness;*
> *he will quiet you by his love;*
> *he will exult over you with loud singing.* (Zephaniah 3:17, ESV)

10

WHY AM I OBSESSED WITH IMPACT?

REAL PURPOSE

A BLACK MAN named George Floyd died due to a white, male cop pinning him to the ground with his knee digging into Floyd's neck, smashing the side of his face into the concrete.

Floyd begged for mercy because he couldn't breathe.

He died.

The nation erupted.

I could feel pain stemming from so many lives.

This black man's family and friends.

This white man's family and friends.

Every cop in the country.

Riots broke out across the nation.

Even in my small-sized city, I could hear the yelling and honking from my doorstep, as I lived on the outskirts of downtown.

My beloved friend, Isaac, came over.

One of the godliest men I know who has rich, deep, radiant ebony skin.

We sat on my steps outside, with the sounds of downtown as the backdrop of our conversation.

We sat there talking until 4:00 AM.

I felt honored to listen to him process his anguish, confusion, and pain.

The following week, I felt weird.

It felt like social media was controlling the entire world.

Thousands and thousands of people posting their opinions without pausing first to examine their own hearts.

I started feeling "blah" about my job.

I started feeling frustrated, lonely, jealous, and unsure.

My mind started wandering into a dangerous place asking,

What the heck am I doing with my life?

I felt like I wasn't doing enough.

I didn't feel like I was serving God radically.

I went for a run.

Even at 8:10 PM the sun was still up since it was summertime.

I had a couple of typical running routes.

Some of which ventured downtown.

It felt unwise due to the ongoing protesting, so I started on a route that stayed in my neighborhood area.

As I jogged I thought I heard,

"Turn around."

I kept running.

I figured it was just coming from my own mind, maybe it was me just wanting to venture downtown to see people and see what was going on.

It wasn't wise to go downtown by myself.

I kept running in the opposite direction.

"Run the other way."

I stopped running and stood there paused on the sidewalk, trying to listen.

I thought and asked,

God, is this really You or just me thinking it? Am I really supposed to run downtown?

I waited a few moments.

I felt an unexplainable deep peace in my spirit.

With faith in my heart and maybe 70% certainty in my brain, I turned around and ran the other way.

Straight toward downtown.

I soon found myself right in the middle of the action.

People everywhere.

People driving and honking with "black lives matter" and "fight for justice " painted on their car windows.

People carrying signs and yelling.

All types of people–old, young, black, white, women, men.

I kept running.

I ran through and past the commotion.

I wasn't really looking for anything intentionally honestly.

I found myself near the apartment I used to live in a few years prior.

Me and my then roommate were confident that God had called us to an apartment complex downtown that was equal opportunity housing.

We didn't qualify to live there because we both made too much money.

But we found out that there were two units in the building that did not fall under the law and went at market rate.

We believed we were supposed to live there and emailed the management almost every other day until we got in.

We only lived there for five months.

Due to bats (yes, the flying kind) that invaded our space, an unsolvable problem which eventually forced us to move. (It was a super cute apartment, though, believe it or not.)

I knew God intentionally had us there even for such a short time.

There is a spot by the entrance where my once neighbors would sit to smoke.

After I moved, whenever I would run by, I would look to see if anyone I knew was out.

As I jogged past, I looked and saw no one initially.

I glanced over at the cute "garden" some of the older ladies would put together each year.

Along a chain-linked fence with a bread factory as its backdrop.

There next to the garden directly behind the dumpster sat a familiar face in an old, plastic chair.

Griffin.

I was thankful I remembered his name.

I ran up to him and stopped, short of breath.

"Griffin, what's up!"

We chatted for a bit and caught up.

As soon as he started talking, I remembered how straightforward he always was.

When I asked how he was doing, he proceeded to tell me that he had been in the hospital for two weeks because he had a boil on his butt that was apparently "eating his flesh."

Well, I appreciated the transparency, HA.

I thought to myself,

Maybe God brought me here because Griffin needed someone to listen to him.

I looked over and an elderly, adorable black woman was watering the plants with a plastic water bottle.

I remembered her.

Griffin reminded me of her name, "Ruth."

The sweet, faithful, 90+ year-old lady who still drove her car to church multiple times a week.

She came over and chatted for a while through her mask, knowing she was one of the most at risk during the coronavirus pandemic.

She left and I chatted with Griffin for a few minutes more and knew I needed to leave because the sun was starting to set and mosquitos were nipping at my legs.

Griffin exclaimed,

"Ah, there's David!"

Good ol' David.

He was the dishwasher at the restaurant below the apartment building.

David would walk past the apartment entrance frequently to take trash to the dumpster.

As he approached the dumpster, I hollered enthusiastically,

"MR. DAVID!"

It had been over a year since I'd seen him last.

He looked up and right away said,

"Miss Fayth!"

I felt so complimented that he remembered my name.

He tossed the garbage bag into the dumpster and with no hesitancy turned around and opened up his arms.

I was sweaty from my run.

He was sweaty from working hard in the kitchen.

We embraced each other right away.

What a cool moment it was considering the nation's current events.

A white, educated, twenty-five-year-old woman.

A black man, in his forties, who washes dishes for a living and has a mental disability.

Remembered each other's names.

And embraced.

David told me and Griffin that he received unemployment while the restaurant closed during the pandemic and how he was happy to be working again.

He also mentioned that he was still available if I was interested.

I kindly said we had a bit of an age gap but that if he would like to be best friends I was totally available.

He accepted.

I said goodbye to my friends and ran back through the protesting to get back home.

~

I walked inside, drank some water, and sat down at my kitchen table.

My mind went back to what I had been struggling with that week.

Wanting to do more things for God.

Wanting to serve more and live out a bigger purpose.

A striking question came to my mind:

Why am I obsessed with impact?

I knew I cared too much about what other people thought about my life and what it looked like.

I wanted to serve more, but was my motivation actually about serving God or about people seeing me serve?

I was so confused.

Was I living out my faith well?

Was I really supposed to be working in the business world?

I just wanted to do more.

In the middle of my mess of confusing thoughts and emotions, I suddenly heard,

"But the dishwasher remembered your name."

My brain's crazy mix of thoughts halted.

But the dishwasher remembered my name...

I cried.

I can sometimes become obsessed with wanting to "do things" for God.

And then I realize that my motivation is off and that the "doing" is actually about me.

Through that simple moment with David, God reminded me that a radical life is living with consistent fruits of the Spirit.

In Galatians 5:22-23, the Apostle Paul tells us that the fruits of the Spirit are love, joy, peace, patience, kindness, goodness, faithfulness, gentleness, and self-control.

This is what changes the world.

Consistent love... consistent faithfulness... consistent kindness...

Given and lived unconditionally.

These fruits of the Spirit need to be lived out in every corner of the world.

In every job.

In every organization.

In every family.

In every community.

For a period of time, I started writing down moments where I encountered Jesus in everyday, "normal" interactions.

Me and my once roommate got pedicures one day and when we left I said,

"If Jesus were to give me a pedicure, I believe it would be like that."

This woman revealed Jesus to me through the way she cared, interacted, and did her work with gentle excellence.

One day, I was on the phone with an insurance lady and she was extremely helpful and kind.

I thanked her and told her how grateful I was for nice, patient insurance people like her because I knew nothing about insurance and needed help.

She responded with her heart,

"You are so welcome, Fayth."

If Jesus were an insurance person on the phone, that's how I would expect Him to respond and sound like.

I hadn't done anything for David.

Our relationship consisted of me walking from my car to the entrance and vice versa.

I said hi.

I asked him a few questions here and there.

Normal, everyday things like how he was doing.

That's it.

I never gave him money.

I never gave him anything.

But in God-reality, I did give him something.

I gave him kindness.

Real, consistent, unconditional kindness.

I communicated to him that I actually saw him and wanted to know his name.

That I cared about who he is.

The "impact" obsession is a lure of Satan to get us fixated on the wrong things.

I often refer to it as being "distracted by the good."

What really impacts the world are people who genuinely love God.

People who are filled with the Holy Spirit.

People who can't help but ooze consistent fruits of the Spirit because they are in love with the One who created the fruit.

People that walk around every day, in normal places, with the glow of

Christ's love in their eyes.

I sometimes overanalyze my whole life based on an obsession with impact.

Forgetting that what makes me shine is my obsession with God.

As a human being,
I might forget again.

> I sometimes overanalyze my whole life based on an obsession with impact. Forgetting that what makes me shine is my obsession with God.

But my prayer is that in that moment, I will hear once again the words whispered,

"But the dishwasher remembered your name."

NOW I can see.

11

STOP ACTING LIKE GROWN UPS

REAL WONDER

I WAS AT my family's lake cottage sitting on the porch reading my Bible.

It was a Sunday morning.

I read Psalm 92 which is titled as "A Song for the Sabbath."

Verses 1-4 read,

> *It is good to give thanks to the Lord,*
> *to sing praises to your name, O Most High;*
> *to declare your steadfast love in the morning,*
> *and your faithfulness by night,*
> *to the music of the lute and the harp,*
> *to the melody of the lyre.*
> *For you, O Lord, have made me glad by your work;*
> *at the works of your hands I sing for joy.* (ESV)

I had a deep desire to dance and sing for God.

I could feel His presence in the warm breeze.

I grabbed my portable speaker from inside and played some worship music.

I somewhat hesitantly walked into the grass and swayed to the music.

In my own home or at church, I wouldn't have even given this a second thought, but since my family was inside, I felt a little awkward.

I wanted to pour myself out to God.

I wanted my family to join me, but I knew they probably wouldn't.

I thought about going to the side of the cottage, out of sight, so that I might worship unashamed and naturally.

I wish I would have had the confidence in that moment to just praise anyways, not caring if anyone joined me or who might watch me.

My eight-year-old cousin walked out onto the front porch and sat down.

I asked him to join me and dance.

I could tell that he wanted to, but I could also see that he was somewhat hesitant because he was embarrassed to join me.

He kept glancing back through the windows to see if anyone was watching from inside.

A saddening thought almost brought tears to my eyes.

He is already starting to lose his wonder.

When I told a friend about this story a few hours later, I wept.

Mourning the fact that I live in a Christian culture that in many ways has seemed to lose its God-wonder.

My cousin was learning from the adults around him, adults who have been conditioned to limit their own wonder.

In his book, *Recapturing the Wonder: Transcendent Faith in a Disenchanted World*, Mike Cosper writes,

"I react to the suggestion of a miracle–or for that matter, any thoughts about God, the spiritual, or the transcendent–with skepticism and cynicism. It is my default setting. I am programmed to expect that the world is what I can see, touch, and measure, any thought or idea that runs against that expectation is met with resistance. Programming is actually a great way to think about it. I have learned to see the world this way, and I don't have to think about it anymore... a disenchanted world has been drained of magic, of any supernatural presences, of spirits and God and transcendence. A disenchanted world is a material world, where what you see is what you get."[19]

My cousin was already starting to become conditioned to believe that instead of dancing in the yard in God-wonder, it would be more comfortable and culturally appropriate to sit inside and watch TV.

Cosper further discusses that once we have learned to see the world in a certain way, we don't really think about it anymore–it's just automatic.

Every day, we can experience the beautiful and tangible mystery of the Gospel and the reality of God's presence.

But to me it seems that most of the people in the world have been conditioned to only live by what one can see with physical eyes.

I love C.S. Lewis and his book series, The Chronicles of Narnia.[20]

In the movie portraying his book, *Prince Caspian: The Return to Narnia*, I noticed a series of dialogues throughout the movie that I believe Lewis included to explain what it means to seek God.[21]

At one point, the four main characters who are siblings and a grumpy dwarf are trying to figure out how to get to a certain destination.

They come to a giant gorge with a river dangerously far below with no way of crossing.

They are about to leave to find another way across when Lucy (the youngest sibling) exclaims,

"It's Aslan! It's Aslan over there! Don't you see! He's right…. there."

When she looks back across the gorge, he's gone.

"Do you see him now?" the dwarf asks doubtfully.

"I'm not crazy. He was there. He wanted us to follow him."

"I'm sure they're any number of lions in this wood…" says the oldest brother, Peter.

"I think I know Aslan when I see him," Lucy responds confidently.

"Look, I'm not about to jump off a cliff after someone who doesn't exist," says

the dwarf.

"The last time I didn't believe Lucy, I ended up looking pretty stupid," responds the youngest brother, Edmund.

"Why wouldn't I have seen him?" Peter asks Lucy.

"Maybe you weren't looking," Lucy responds gently.

Aslan, a lion, symbolizes God.

What Lucy sees, the others didn't, *because they weren't looking.*

The group then attempts a different route, only to find it fully occupied by enemy soldiers.

They travel back to where Lucy said she spotted Aslan.

"So where exactly do you think you saw Aslan?" Peter asks.

What Lucy sees, the others didn't, because they weren't looking.

Lucy glances around at the doubtful faces around her.

"I wish you'd all stop trying to sound like grown-ups. I don't think I saw him, I did see him," states Lucy.

"I... am a grown up," says the little dwarf.

Some comic relief.

Lucy wanders to the cliff's edge and says,

"It was right over…"

The cliff's edge suddenly collapses underneath Lucy's feet as she shrieks.

"LUCY!" yells Susan, the oldest sister, as they all sprint to try to save her.

They look down to see Lucy sitting safely on a patch of land they wouldn't have known was there had she not fallen through and landed on it.

This unseen part of the gorge led to a trail that safely brought them down and across to the other side.

———

Lucy acted on her faith even though the others doubted what she had seen.

And then out of nowhere, she was shown a clear path.

———

Later that evening, they are sleeping under the stars next to a fire.

Susan and Lucy both lie awake next to one another.

"Lucy, are you awake?" Susan whispers.

"Mhmm."

"Why do you think I didn't see Aslan?" Susan asks.

"You believe me," Lucy states, surprised.

"Well, we got across the gorge."

"I don't know," Lucy pauses to think.

"Maybe you didn't really want to."

Lucy was unsure as to why Susan didn't see Aslan, too.

All she knew was that she desperately wanted to see Aslan and that his presence was real.

She wasn't sure if her siblings felt the same.

Days later, Peter sits next to Lucy and says,

"You're lucky, you know."

"What do you mean?" asks Lucy.

"To have seen him. I wish he would just give me some sort of proof."

"Maybe we're the ones who need to prove ourselves to him," Lucy gently responds.

Lucy recognized that Aslan was consistent and always there.

She didn't need to see a miracle or some sort of sign to know Aslan was alive and would come soon.

Lucy knew it was her role to believe, obey, and expect.

⌒

The siblings and the dwarf eventually find their way to the others they were searching for.

The enemy soon arrives for battle and they try to figure out how they can defend themselves.

"*...that's your next big plan. Sending a little girl into the darkest parts of the forest alone?*" questions the dwarf.

"*It's our only chance,*" Peter responds.

"*And she won't be alone,*" says Susan who would accompany Lucy.

"*Haven't enough of us died already?*" says the dwarf out of fear for Lucy.

"*Nikabrik* [who doubted and embraced evil] *was my friend too. But he lost hope. Queen Lucy hasn't and neither have I,*" says a brave badger.

Lucy rides into the woods while the others try to hold off the enemy.

Susan jumps off the horse to take down some unexpected soldiers so Lucy can continue on alone.

Lucy rides her horse as fast as she can while an enemy soldier chases her.

Aslan suddenly appears, scaring Lucy's horse onto its hind feet.

Lucy falls to the ground.

Aslan takes down the soldier with ease.

"*Aslan!*"

Lucy runs to the lion and hugs him to the ground.

"*I knew it was you! The whole time I knew it. But the others didn't believe me,*" exclaims Lucy.

"**And why would that stop you from coming to me?**"

Lucy pauses.

"*I'm sorry, I was too scared to come alone.*"

<hr />

With no other options, they sent Lucy into the woods having no idea if it was even a possibility for Aslan to show up.

When Lucy *intentionally* goes to find Aslan, she finds him.

She tells him that she knew he was always there but she didn't go to him because the others didn't believe her.

She didn't want to be alone.

Other people's doubt caused Lucy to abstain from going to find Aslan.

<hr />

Lucy and Aslan chat for a bit, and then Aslan says he will help with the battle.

"*Oh, I wish I was braver,*" says Lucy.

"If you were any braver, you would be a lioness," Aslan responds with a chuckle.

What made Lucy brave was her faith.

Aslan wipes out the enemy.

Peace is restored in the land.

With the battle won and wounds being tended to, Aslan asks Lucy about the dwarf who doubted him.

"Now, where is this dear little friend you've told me so much about?" asks Aslan.

The dwarf hesitantly walks up to Aslan and kneels before him.

Aslan roars a great roar, the power of his breath fanning back the dwarf's long beard.

He shuts his eyes tightly and shudders.

"Do you see him now?" asks Lucy with an "I-told-you-so" yet sweet tone.

Aslan smiles at the dwarf with a fatherly grin.

Lucy could see Aslan before anything came to fruition.

The dwarf only believed after the battle was won, when he could physically see Aslan.

～

To see and experience God, we have to stop acting like grown-ups.

We have to stop pretending like we know what we're doing and where we're going.

To see, we have to seek.

With undoubting faith.

Why do we often complicate it so much?

Jeremiah 29:13 states,

> *You will seek me and find me, when you seek me with all your heart.* (ESV)

Verses 13-14 in The Message version words it like this:

> *When you come looking for me, you'll find me. Yes, when you get serious about finding me and want it more than anything else, I'll make sure you won't be disappointed...*

～

In the Old Testament, David was a chosen king of God.

He was a great, mighty, strategic leader.

Jesus Christ was born through his lineage.

The Bible tells us that David worshiped God and danced in the streets in God's presence before his people.

The Bible says he was wearing a "linen ephod" which some believe to be similar to a loin cloth. If he was wearing just this or more, we can't really know for sure.

Regardless, we do know his wife was not pleased and embarrassed with David's behavior.

The ark of the covenant, the symbol for the presence of God, was brought into David's city.

It had been stolen by the enemy, the Philistines, and it had been gone for twenty years.

> *And David danced before the Lord with all his might. And David was wearing a linen ephod. So David and all the house of Israel brought up the ark of the Lord with shouting and with the sound of the horn. As the ark of the Lord came into the city of David, Michal the daughter of Saul looked out of the window and saw King David leaping and dancing before the Lord, and she despised him in her heart.* (2 Samuel 6:14-16, ESV)

David's wife was mad when she saw him and scolded him for doing such a thing.

> *David returned home to bless his family. Michal, Saul's daughter, came out to greet him: "How wonderfully the king has distinguished himself today—exposing himself to the eyes of the servants' maids like some burlesque street dancer!" David replied to Michal, "**In God's presence I'll dance all I want!** He chose me over your father and the rest of our family and made me prince over God's people, over Israel. **Oh yes, I'll dance to God's glory—more recklessly even**

than this. And as far as I'm concerned... I'll gladly look like a fool... but among these maids you're so worried about, I'll be honored no end." (2 Samuel 6:20-22, MSG, emphasis added)

The most powerful people in the world are the ones who are unafraid to show their affection for God.

Regardless of what others might think.

⌒

May I never withhold my affection from the Lord.

Whether people believe me or if they don't.

Whether people join me or if they don't.

Whether people choose to seek or if they don't.

Whether I am praised or judged.

Whether I am alone or with others.

May I always dance in His presence unashamed.

May I model faith and wonder for generations to come.

May I not just tell people to "rejoice in the Lord," but with my mind, body, and spirit, actually rejoice in the Lord!

⌒

One way to define *wonder* is "rapt attention or astonishment at something awesomely mysterious or new to one's experience."[22]

How will I do this and grow in it practically?

After I run on a clear day, I will sit next to the river for a few minutes and gaze at the moon against the bright blue sky and linger in solitude.

When I have the window seat on a plane, I will play worship music in my headphones and glance out over the world, captivated that such creation is possible and such a Creator could be present with me.

When the sun starts to set and the golden glow starts to radiate throughout my apartment, I will stop what I'm doing for a moment, look, and sing whatever is in my heart.

When I'm driving on a warm day, I will roll my windows down, blare a favorite worship song, raise a hand through the sunroof, notice everything around me, and linger.

I see a vision–one where the straight-lined, scared-to-raise-their-hands churchgoers transform into a group of Holy Spirit-dependent God lovers who dance in His presence with shameless adoration in their everyday lives.

It's time to stop acting like grown-ups.

It's time to joyfully live out our role as dependent children.

It's time to not seek God just when we are in trouble,

But to expect and want to see Him every day of our lives.

It's time for me to dance on the lawn, unashamed of who might be watching.

Because in God's presence, I'll dance all I want.

Even if people think I look like a fool.

NOW I can see.

> *Truly, I say to you, unless you turn and become like children, you will never enter the kingdom of heaven.* (Matthew 18:3, ESV)

"May we never lose our wonder
Wide eyed and mystified
May we be just like a child
Staring at the beauty of our King"

—WONDER | BETHEL MUSIC[23]

12

LISTENING IS LIFE

REAL LEADERSHIP

I WAS SUPER stressed.

I was working from home, trying to figure out how to meet my deadlines.

I had a contractor, Lindsey, that was working for me part time.

A dear friend whom I had worked with before at a different company.

She was only a couple years younger than me.

I didn't feel like I was leading her well at all.

We had a phone call the day prior where she cried because she was so stressed.

I felt so bad and didn't feel like I had the time or tools to really help her.

⁓

Outside my window, I saw what looked like a lady trying to deliver flowers.

I lived in a house that was split into four apartments so the entrances were confusing for anyone delivering mail.

She headed for the door that went to the upstairs apartments.

I had a brief moment of jealousy.

One of the ladies who lived above me must be getting flowers from her significant other.

Must be nice.

The lady looked very confused and backed away from the entrance.

I opened up my window to help her and explained that the entrances are confusing and asked who she was looking for.

"I am looking for apartment one."

"I'm apartment one!" I responded with surprised excitement.

I told her to meet me on the other side of the house where my entrance was.

She handed me a beautiful, very green (my favorite color) arrangement of plants.

I thanked her and walked back inside.

Who the heck would have sent these?

I had no idea. Maybe my dad?

I sat them down on my counter and opened up the little card that came with the arrangement.

THANKS FOR ALWAYS LISTENING. SO GRATEFUL FOR FRIENDS LIKE YOU.

LOVE, LINDSEY

I was stunned.

So completely touched.

I took a picture right away and texted it to her with overwhelming thanks.

I thought I wasn't doing a good job with Lindsey.

And then she sent me a gorgeous plant arrangement *because I listened to her.*

This simple yet extremely impactful moment reminded me that listening is one of the most powerful things in the world.

> It reminded me that real leaders are the ones who listen first.

It reminded me that real leaders are the ones who listen first.

Leaders that listen with their hearts.

We might not always have the right words to say or know the right thing to do to make a situation better, but we always have the power to attentively listen and show that we deeply care.

~

This moment made me think of verse 19 in the first chapter of James which says we are to be *"quick to listen, slow to speak, and slow to get angry"* (NLT).

In our day-to-day lives, we are to be intentional listeners.

Not only with other people, but with God.

When we are quick to listen and slow to speak, we create room for other voices.

When we are intentionally still in the presence of the Lord, we create room for Him to speak to us clearly.

~

I ended up splitting up all of the plants included in the arrangement and individually repotted them.

This reminder is now planted, placed, and growing in various spots in my home.

A reminder that listening is life.

NOW I can see.

When we are quick to listen and slow to speak, we create room for other voices.

13

WHAT DID YOU DO TODAY?

REAL PRODUCTIVITY

IT WAS ABOUT noon on a summer Saturday.

My coworker/friend texted me to see if I was home because he was at a nearby coffee shop with his four boys.

We had worked together for about three years and I had heard so many stories about his boys but had never met them.

I was excited when they stopped by.

They stayed in their car (as this was during the coronavirus pandemic) and I popped out of my apartment to chat.

The kids were so adorable–all under the age of ten, blabbing one hundred miles per hour and telling me jokes.

My coworker was simply making conversation when he asked,

"So what have you done so far today?"

It's sad how quickly I felt some sort of weird shame and felt like I had to have a list of things to say.

The worldly part of me wanted to say something like,

"I went for a run, had a coffee date with a friend, and now I'm getting ready to leave to spend time with family."

But that wasn't true that day.

"Not much," I heard myself say.

"When you texted I was spending some time with the Lord."

I could hear the lack of confidence in my voice.

We talked for a few more minutes.

They left.

A few questions nagged at me right away.

Why do I feel lame when I don't have a list of things to say when people ask me about my day?

And why was I hesitant when I said I was spending time with the Lord? He is a believer!

I believe Satan often tempts us with busyness.

He has twisted our culture into one that is obsessed with having a full schedule.

It seems like, unfortunately, this trickery has been pretty effective.

I think of when Jesus was in the home of Mary and Martha many years ago, told in Luke 10.

These two sisters each made a choice when Jesus visited their home.

Mary decided to literally sit at Jesus' feet.

She sat there and just listened to Him and looked at His face.

She positioned herself to see Him.

Martha chose something else.

She chose to make a meal for Jesus.

To get everything ready to serve Jesus well.

The passage says she was distracted.

It was probably a lot harder to hear Jesus from the kitchen.

She got upset because her sister wasn't helping her make the preparations.

Jesus told Martha that she was worried and upset over all the details when there was only one thing worth being concerned about.

He said that Mary had made the better choice.

And that this choice would never be taken away from her.

I can be tempted to be like Martha sometimes.

Wanting to serve Jesus so well and wanting to do good things to the point where I neglect the most important thing of all, just being with Him.

When Satan tries to get us off the path God has us on, it's not like he throws a giant bus in the middle of the path and we see it and we're like QUICK! A BUS FELL IN THE ROAD, RUN AROUND IT!

Satan is extremely intelligent.

And he knows who God is.

Satan will do everything he can with the little power that he has to get us to be fixated on anything other than God.

And he does this strategically.

The things he tempts us with often *look godly*.

He tries to twist the narrative so that we feel like we are doing good things, distracting us from living out the specific good things God planned for us.

He keeps going in an effort to get us so busy with doing all of these "good things" that eventually lead to Satan gaining his greatest victory of all–us becoming so distracted that we neglect sitting at Jesus' feet.

Satan tries to cut us off from our very source of life.

He tries to keep us busy in the noisy kitchen, so that we cannot hear Jesus' voice or see His face clearly.

As we get busier and busier and spend time with God less and less, our sense of joy, rest, peace, clarity, confidence, and contentment start to fade.

And sometimes we are completely unaware this is happening, thinking that we are doing the right things.

It makes me sad that I felt any shame when I told my coworker I was spending time with the Lord.

Like I had to prove myself through the tasks of the day.

When in reality I was doing the most productive, insane, supernatural thing one can experience while in this temporary world.

I was spending intimate time with God.

I was communicating with the Creator of the universe.

And I had almost felt embarrassed.

As Bill Johnson, Senior Leader of Bethel Church, once stated,

"Busyness is artificial significance."[24]

There's nothing wrong with doing good things, but doing good things just for the sake of doing good things means nothing.

Filling our schedules just for the sake of having a full schedule means nothing.

Our *doing* has to come out of a place of *being*.

Being has to be first, and *doing* second.

The next time someone asks me about my day's events after I have spent a long period of time with the Lord...

I will answer with confidence.

NOW I can see.

14

I FEEL IT EVERY DAY

REAL COMMUNION

IT WAS EARLIER on during the coronavirus pandemic.

Indiana had just started to open back up to allow small gatherings.

I went to a small party with my siblings and some friends.

Two days afterward while I was working from home, I received a text from a friend who was at the party letting me and multiple others know that she tested positive for the virus.

At this point in the pandemic, it wasn't as common to know people who had it.

I hadn't experienced anything personally until then.

In a moment, things felt much more real.

I paused.

I got on my knees and prayed for myself, my siblings, my friends, and everyone else I had come in contact with since the party.

I texted each of them to let them know what happened.

Meanwhile, the group text my infected friend had started was erupting with messages.

People asking what everyone was planning to do, some stating they were going to get tested right away.

Some had to because of their jobs.

I thanked God that I was still working from home and hadn't seen my coworkers or any clients.

I knew God would let me know if I needed to take any additional action.

A question popped into my mind a couple hours later:

Why don't we always go to God first?

I can remember when I used to go to other people first before going to God.

Sometimes I still do.

Instead of asking Him first, I might go to another person or take immediate action doing what I think is right.

But I know in my heart the wisest, most powerful, and most effective thing I can do is to ask God immediately with intentionality.

I trust the Holy Spirit will speak to me.

I continued working.

I had music playing.

A song popped on that caught my attention.

"No Fear" by Laney Rene.[25]

The song reminded me of some questions I had been asked recently.

"How do you hear God?"

"What does His voice sound like?"

"How do you know?"

One of the verses of the song reads,

You have captured my attention
With such beauty on display
I can feel Your affection
I feel it every day

This brought to mind why I believed I could hear God's voice more clearly than I had used to.

I wasn't paying as close of attention before.

The more I learned to still myself in the presence of God, the easier it became to hear Him speak to me.

The easier it became to feel His affection on a daily basis.

~

I believe one of the biggest lies the enemy tries to throw at people is that they cannot hear God.

That they are not good enough for God to speak to them.

That other people might be able to hear God, but they never will.

This is just a straight up lie.

None of us are worthy of God's attention.

That's why God sent Jesus to be a sacrifice for us.

So that even in our sin, we might draw near to Him.

So that we could have a relationship with Him.

There is no formula for hearing God's voice except for this: *be with Him.*

The more I acknowledged and invited God into my everyday moments, the more I realized His affection for me.

A mutual delight which led to consistent back and forth communication throughout the day.

Not a relationship where I get on my knees three times a day

There is no formula for hearing God's voice except for this: be with Him.

to "say a prayer" at Him, but a steady flow of communication where I can share anything and everything with Him.

~

He speaks into the small and big moments of life–and everything in between.

I might be leaving my home and having an illogical OCD moment, afraid I left an appliance on and my house will burn down while I'm gone, HA.

And God whispers, *"Go in peace, daughter"* and I feel so much better about leaving.

It blows me away that He cares–even about such a silly, typical-human moment like that.

When I co-led a trip in Asia, I had a moment where I found myself with ten students completely lost.

My phone had no signal and I didn't know what to do.

I was looking at my phone, pretending to be doing something, and asked God what I should do.

I was pretty sure God said,

"Go this way, daughter."

With a mixture of anxiety and faith in my heart, I led the group and walked in the direction I heard Him say.

A few minutes later, my phone gained signal.

God, of course, doesn't just speak into times of fear, but into times of joy.

Often I will wake up on a slow Saturday morning, roll over to see the golden sunshine streaming through the blinds, whisper good morning to God and hear,

"Good morning, My sweet one."

I might accomplish a big task for work and thank the Lord for helping me and hear,

"Well done, My dear one."

And it goes way farther than this!

We can ask Him questions.

We can process with Him.

We can tell Him everything.

I realize now that God has been speaking to me my entire life.

I just genuinely was not paying attention or spending real time with Him.

I wasn't acknowledging His presence.

I hear Him now because I am listening and I expect to hear Him.

This level of closeness is available to everyone.

The chorus of the song reads,

I have no fear
When I look at You
I have no fear
When my eyes are on You
I have no fear
When I look into Your face
I don't have to be afraid

So this is why my fear was minimal the morning I found out I was exposed to the virus.

My fear has become pretty minimal because I've learned to make trusting Him my first response.

To trust His voice before anyone else's.

This is not always, or perhaps ever, a flawless experience.

I can still be tempted to be fearful and can start to slip, but I literally say to myself,

"Flex your trust muscles, Fayth."

I have to lock my eyes with God's as best I can.

I can be like Peter, Jesus' disciple, when he lost faith walking on the water because he didn't stay focused on Jesus.

The disciples were in a boat in a storm when Jesus came to them walking on top of the sea.

Naturally, the disciples were freaked out and thought it might be a ghost.

Jesus told them it was Him and not to be afraid.

Peter stated,

> Lord, if it is you, command me to come to you on the water.
> (Matthew 14:28, ESV)

Jesus told Peter to come.

Peter started to walk, glanced at the scary wind, became afraid, and began to sink.

He called out to Jesus to save him and Jesus immediately takes hold of Peter and says,

> O you of little faith, why did you doubt? (Matthew 14:31, ESV)

The more I know the Lord and His voice, the more illogical fear becomes.

⁓

Several people asked me if I was going to get tested for the virus.

I felt peace that I didn't need to.

This may have looked foolish to some.

> The more I know the Lord and His voice, the more illogical fear becomes.

This led me to think about what wisdom really means.

The world says that wisdom in that moment would be to do what the experts recommended and perhaps to get tested immediately.

I am all about being wise and exercising caution for the good of others and myself.

But this situation caused me to reflect on the difference between how the world defines wisdom and how God defines wisdom.

One way to define the word *wisdom* is,

"Accumulated philosophical or scientific learning: KNOWLEDGE."[26]

So then, a wise person in the world's eyes is someone who knows a lot of facts... statistics... science... etc.

God explains wisdom differently.

Proverbs 1:7 reads,

> *The fear of the Lord is the beginning of knowledge; fools despise wisdom and instruction.* (ESV)

The Message version words it like this:

> *Start with God—**the first step in learning is bowing to God**; only fools thumb their noses at such wisdom and learning.* (emphasis added)

James 1:5 reads,

> *If any of you lacks wisdom, **let him ask God**, who gives generously to all without reproach, and it will be given to him.* (ESV, emphasis added)

The Message version words it like this:

*If you don't know what you're doing, pray to the Father. **He loves to help**. You'll get his help, and won't be condescended to when you ask for it.* (emphasis added)

This seems pretty clear to me.

When something happens or when I don't know what I'm doing (which is often, LOL), real, effective wisdom is going to God first before going to anything or anyone else.

And when I do this in faith, He will answer.

To hear His voice, we have to believe that He can speak to us.

And even in our struggle to believe, we can ask Him to help us believe.

His grace and patience is unending.

In every situation–whether it be difficult, painful, scary, exciting, or joyful–may I communicate with God first.

No matter what pandemics or earthly events may come,

May I trust His voice.

Every day.

NOW I can see.

My sheep hear my voice, and I know them, and they follow me. I give them eternal life, and they will never perish, and no one will snatch them out of my hand. (John 10:27-28, ESV)

But let him ask in faith, with no doubting, for the one who doubts is like a wave of the sea that is driven and tossed by the wind. (James 1:6, ESV)

15

OWN YOUR BELOVEDNESS

REAL DELIGHT

I WAS GRIEVING for my dad.

I could see the longing in him.

With everything, he wanted God fully.

He was deeply rooted in God's Word for hours every day.

But something was constricting him from fully *experiencing* God.

He has a lot of deep scars from his past.

Scars I don't think he is even fully aware of.

From my perspective, he has conditioned himself to not feel certain things because he had to in order to cope growing up.

For so many years, he hadn't experienced unconditional love.

I can see in my dad the deep lie that he has to *do something* in order to be loved.

It breaks me.

Because I cherish my dad with everything I am.

And I would not be who I am or where I am without him.

If only he could see himself the way that I see him.

I have written him countless letters and poems, told him with my voice over and over, given him meaningful gifts, sang for him...

And he just never seems to fully grasp how radiant he is.

Which I believe restricts him from fully experiencing God.

I heard a song I hadn't heard before and it brought me to tears.

It made me think of my dad.

"Belovedness" by Sarah Kroger.[27]

You've owned your fear and all your self-loathing
You've owned the voices inside of your head
You've owned the shame and reproach of your failure
It's time to own your belovedness

You've owned your past and how it's defined you

You've owned everything everybody else says
It's time to hear what your Father has spoken
It's time to own your belovedness

He says, "You're mine, I smiled when I made you
I find you beautiful in every way
My love for you is fierce and unending
I'll come to find you, whatever it takes
My beloved"

You've owned the mess you see in the mirror
You've owned the lies that you're just not enough
You've been so blinded by all you're comparing
It's time to own your belovedness

My dad needed to own his belovedness.

He needed to stop owning the lies of the past and grip with his heart the reality of God's love for him.

Not just agreeing with words, but agreeing with his spirit, his entire being.

In the movie *The Perks of Being a Wallflower*, a specific line struck me:

"*We accept the love we think we deserve.*"[28]

We so often settle for less, because that's what we think we're worth.

Our decisions reflect what we believe we deserve.

How much or how little we value ourselves.

We often, perhaps unknowingly, stop goodness from coming into our lives because we don't believe with our hearts that we are worth it.

In his book, *The Purpose Driven Life: What on Earth Am I Here For?*, Rick Warren writes my favorite quote concerning humility:

"Humility is not thinking less of yourself; it is thinking of yourself less."[29]

We have every reason to be beautifully confident in who we are and everything God has created us to be.

We can be humble and confident at the same time.

I started experiencing God more fully when I grasped that I truly love who I am.

When I owned it.

When I owned that I am legitimately His beloved.

I was never able to fully delight in God's presence until I fully grasped my radiant, glowing worth.

Not because of anything I've done or not done, but simply because God designed me.

Without Him, I am nothing.

But with Him, I am everything.

> I started experiencing God more fully when I grasped that I truly love who I am.

I realized that owning my belovedness is what makes rejoicing in God to the fullest possible.

It's hard for me to comprehend, but I know God consistently delights in me.

Even in my sin and countless imperfections.

He continues to choose me.

> Without Him, I am nothing.
> But with Him, I am everything.

He freely gives me grace and continues to pursue me anyway.

What incomprehensible wonder.

I also realized owning my belovedness is what allowed me to start loving others for real–a pure, fierce love that is not self-seeking–because I don't need humans to fill some void inside me.

I'm already full.

But how do we own it?

What does it mean to practically own our belovedness?

We can write God's Word about us down and meditate on it over and over and over.

I praise you, for I am fearfully and wonderfully made... (Psalm 139:14, ESV)

If anyone is in Christ, he is a new creation. The old has passed away; behold, the new has come. (2 Corinthians 5:17, ESV)

Charm is deceptive, and beauty is fleeting; but a woman who fears the Lord is to be praised. (Proverbs 31:30, NIV)

We can write an identity statement and proclaim it over ourselves, over and over and over.

I, Fayth Glock, am a beautiful, loved, forgiven, truth-filled, joy-bound, awe-inspired daughter of the Most High.

We have to declare over ourselves who we are.

We have to remind ourselves daily of our own worth.

But most importantly, the way we fully start to experience the reality of our belovedness is through sitting still with God, giving Him the space to pour His affection over us.

It's hard to tell a toddler that is running around the living room and screaming that you love them.

But as soon as they *choose* to jump into your arms and let you hold them, you can hug them close and lovingly whisper your deep affection and love over the child.

But most importantly, the way we fully start to experience the reality of our belovedness is through sitting still with God, giving Him the space to pour His affection over us.

An unconditional love that has nothing to do with the child's behavior.

It's time.

For my dad, for all of us.

To stop owning the lies and, instead, own our imperishable beauty.

So many people are not experiencing God the way they long to because they are not fully accepting their God-given value.

I see so many people who love God genuinely, but are not fully letting God love them!

They're owning everything else, like the song says: fear, self-loathing, shame, failures, comparison…

It's time to own why Jesus came.

He not only died for our salvation, but also to set us free from self-condemnation.

It's time for us to pour ourselves out before God.

To let go.

To let ourselves break.

> He not only died for our salvation, but also to set us free from self-condemnation.

To be real.

To fall into His arms after so many years of running and screaming.

To just let Him hold us and whisper over us–His beloved children.

NOW I can see.

I will be glad and rejoice in your unfailing love,
for you have seen my troubles,
and you care about the anguish of my soul. (Psalm 31:7, NLT)

Therefore humble yourselves under the mighty hand of God [set aside self-righteous pride], so that He may exalt you [to a place of honor in His service] at the appropriate time, casting all your cares [all your anxieties, all your worries, and all your concerns, once and for all] on Him, for He cares about you [with deepest affection, and watches over you very carefully]. (1 Peter 5:6-7, AMP)

As the Father has loved me, so have I loved you. Abide in my love. (John 15:9, ESV)

See how very much our Father loves us, for he calls us his children, and that is what we are! But the people who belong to this world don't recognize that we are God's children because they don't know him. (1 John 3:1, NLT)

16

FOR WHAT?

REAL ENDURANCE

I WAS HONESTLY in some sort of agony.

For about a month, I went to bed with tears running down my face and a headache every night.

But somehow, I was genuinely thankful at the same time.

It helped me so much when a friend told me that it is completely possible to genuinely hold and experience contradicting emotions.

Even though I was going to bed with tears down my face, I still felt near to the Lord.

I was crying with Him, I guess?

It was so confusing, but also somehow made sense.

I had been working from home alone for months because of the coronavirus pandemic.

I was lonely and I felt embarrassed to admit it.

I was tired and worn out from work.

I was carrying a lot of weight for several people in my life in really difficult situations.

I was feeling jealous.

Painful, old memories were resurfacing.

I was feeling like things were unfair.

One evening, I was video chatting with my mom while making dinner.

I for sure was not in the best place that night.

I was venting and asking the question,

"For what?"

Why was I doing what I was doing?

Why had I always tried to choose obedience to God before what I wanted?

Had I gained anything from it?

Look where it had gotten me.

I didn't want to talk to my mom anymore.

I said a quick goodbye and hung up.

~

I was listening to one of my favorite Christian YouTubers, Oboitshepo Tladi, the next day.[30]

She referenced Revelation 3:8-13 and the words hit me deeply.

I looked up the passage in The Message version:

> *I see what you've done. Now see what I've done.* I've opened a door before you that no one can slam shut. You don't have much strength, I know that; you used what you had to keep my Word. You didn't deny me when times were rough. And watch as I take those who call themselves true believers but are nothing of the kind, pretenders whose true membership is in the club of Satan—watch as I strip off their pretensions and they're forced to acknowledge it's you that I've loved. *Because you kept my Word in passionate patience*, I'll keep you safe in the time of testing that will be here soon, and all over the earth, every man, woman, and child put to the test. I'm on my way; I'll be there soon. *Keep a tight grip on what you have so no one distracts you and steals your crown.* I'll make each conqueror a pillar in the sanctuary of my God, a permanent position of honor. Then I'll write names on you, the pillars: the Name of my God, the Name of God's City—the new Jerusalem coming down out of Heaven—and my new Name. Are your ears awake? Listen. Listen to the Wind Words, the Spirit blowing through the churches. (emphasis added)

I texted the Scripture to my mom.

She responded right away.

"This is the answer to what you were saying last night."

She was right.

I knew I was living for more than the earth.

I knew in my heart that I was living for way more than the traditional milestones my culture glamorized.

But I had lost sight.

I had drifted and needed to refocus once again.

Back to eternal instead of temporary.

My beloved friend, Isaac, had given me a prophetic vision a few months prior.

One particular thing he said really stuck out to me.

He was talking about people living their earthly lives for the Lord:

*"Some people do things for God out of fear or obligation, but you **can't not** do things for God because of your deep, real love for Him."*

I knew in my heart he was right, regardless of my hesitancy.

Even with the anguish and frustration I sometimes feel, I knew this was genuinely true.

I can't not.

Not because of any sort of obligation or fear.

But because I love Him and I know His unconditional love for me.

And out of this I know my obedience ultimately comes.

I'm sure so many people in the Bible experienced this anguish in their hearts.

Noah had to think it was unfair that he had to spend a lot of his life building a giant boat that seemed to make no sense, watch the entire human race die, and then try to survive in nature when everything had been wiped out.

Sure, he and his family survived.

But there is not one part of this story that would have been enjoyable, and he was deemed a blameless and righteous man.

Job was totally obedient and literally had all of his wealth and family taken away from him just because God told Satan that He knew Job would still be faithful even if he didn't have all the blessings.

From Job's perspective, he must have felt he was being punished for no reason.

Jeremiah was super obedient and lived most of his life as a faithful prophet, delivering condemning and harsh prophetic messages.

Oftentimes this resulted in physical suffering and rejection, to the point he said he wished he had never been born.

Talk about loneliness.

Yet he wrote in Jeremiah 15:16,

> *Your words were found, and I ate them,*
> *and your words became to me a joy*
> *and the delight of my heart,*
> *for I am called by your name, O Lord, God of hosts.* (ESV)

And above all, Jesus Christ Himself–who lived a sinless, perfect life–was tortured and killed.

—

Obedience to God does not always result in what we think it should.

The ones that are faithful to the point of death understand that obedience has everything to do with who God is, and not about earthly outcomes.

I choose to listen and be obedient to God because I love Him.

And when things don't look like what I think they should...

I have to trust Him and know that I was made for more than this short period of time on earth.

—

I decided to go on a run the day after the call with my mom.

I walked outside and it was absolutely gorgeous: 75 degrees, sunny, a warm breeze.

The sky was stunningly blue.

I ran up the hill to the trail and started to run alongside the river.

A new song I had been recently listening to, "I'd Pick You" by Praytell, was streaming through my headphones.[31]

It was a love song.

One that made me long for a husband, to be held by a man.

The ones that are faithful to the point of death understand that obedience has everything to do with who God is, and not about earthly outcomes.

But I realized I needed to switch the context to God.

I looked up to my left and saw a plane leaving a long, white trail in the sky.

I looked forward, and a small rainbow floated above me–God's symbol of promise.

The lyrics streamed through my headphones:

"I'd pick you, all over again. A million times. Start over and then. I'd pick you. All over again."

I cried.

The Lord caught my attention on that average day.

I thought back to my words,

"For what?"

Because He had chosen me.

He picked me.

And I'll always pick Him.

NOW I can see.

> *And whoever does not take his cross and follow me is not worthy of me. Whoever finds his life will lose it, and whoever loses his life for my sake will find it.* (Matthew 10:38-39, ESV)

> *And let us not grow weary of doing good, for in due season we will reap, if we do not give up.* (Galatians 6:9, ESV)

17

I WILL DANCE WEIRD, NOW

REAL JOY

I WAS HOME by myself.

I was so thankful for a day of rest.

The work week had been hectic.

I did some Christmas shopping for my family.

I repotted some plants.

I cleaned.

I didn't have any plans.

I galloped from my desk to the kitchen, singing.

I did a random, spinning dance move.

Once in the kitchen I made a weird, giddy "Fayth-sound" and did some sort of strange, awesome jump.

I laughed to myself.

A strong thought hit me:

My joy has nothing to do with other people.

⁓

I've always been a pretty joyful person.

I realized how real my joy was while I was living alone and working from home for months during the coronavirus pandemic.

Real, genuine joy has nothing to do with what's happening or what's not, what I have or what I don't have.

That silly moment struck me with the legit heart belief that no matter what my life looks like throughout my years, I can dance.

As a single person, I can dance content.

If I get married someday, I can dance content.

Alone, I can dance content.

Surrounded by friends, I can dance content.

In a boring cubicle, I can dance content.

In a dream job, I can dance content.

Whether in bliss or pain, I can still dance content.

Forever... I can dance content and do weird jumps.

Because I know God.

And He knows me.

I for sure have my moments of sadness and frustration, but in the depths of my heart the supernatural joy is always there.

Because joy is not an emotion or a fleeting feeling.

It's a God-given fruit of the Spirit that we can choose if we continuously abide in the Holy Spirit.

Unexplainable, incomprehensible joy is found in His presence.

Every period of life has something in it to be cherished.

Whenever a big life change happens, there's usually something we mourn that we lose, no matter how happy we are about the new things that come.

"The grass is always greener" quote couldn't be more true.

If we live life waiting for new grass, we'll never dance in the grass we're in.

Which would result in a life where we never dance.

So I will dance weird, *now.*

Because that's what real joy is.

Real joy is anywhere.

Real joy is Him.

Real joy is now.

NOW I can see.

> *You make known to me the path of life;*
> *in your presence there is fullness of joy;*
> *at your right hand are pleasures forevermore.* (Psalm 16:11, ESV)

> *Joyful are people of integrity,*
> *who follow the instructions of the Lord.*
> *Joyful are those who obey his laws*
> *and search for him with all their hearts.*
> *They do not compromise with evil,*
> *and they walk only in his paths.* (Psalm 119:1-3, NLT)

> *You did it: you changed wild lament*
> *into whirling dance;*
> *You ripped off my black mourning band*
> *and decked me with wildflowers.*
> *I'm about to burst with song;*
> *I can't keep quiet about you.*
> *God, my God,*
> *I can't thank you enough.* (Psalm 30:11-12, MSG)

"The holy grail of joy is not in some exotic location or some emotional mountain peak experience. The joy wonder could be here! Here, in the messy, piercing ache of now, joy might be—unbelievably—possible."

—ANN VOSKAMP | ONE THOUSAND GIFTS[32]

18

I WOULDN'T TRADE IT FOR ANYTHING

REAL FULFILLMENT

I WAS ON a video call with my mom.

We were having one of our daily chats about anything and everything.

The topic of marriage came up.

My mom said something that rocked my perspective:

"Fayth, you know I love your dad. But what you have with God... your intimacy with Him... I wouldn't trade for anything."

I immediately responded.

"No, I wouldn't trade it for anything."

The words kept coming back to me all day.

I loved how my mom as a married woman and I as a single woman both knew we wanted God more.

I wouldn't trade my intimacy with God for absolutely anything.

Nothing.

Not one dream.

And I realized in that moment with my mom… that I actually meant it.

One night, God gave me a dream.

I was standing on the edge of a lake.

Three piers were before me.

At the end of the first pier was a large group of my family and closest friends.

At the end of the second pier stood a man representing a God-given husband.

At the end of the last pier stood Jesus.

I was told to walk to the end of the pier of my choosing.

It was made clear that I could only choose one.

I didn't hesitate to turn away from my family, friends, and man of my dreams.

To walk straight to Jesus.

Even though my longings for things on earth can be super deep, I know that I thirst for God more.

We live in a world and culture that screams at us to be discontent.

To want more.

But I know...

I know.

That my ultimate dream and fulfillment has already been attained.

If my earthly life were to stay like it is right now forever...

Same job.

Same income.

Same relationship status.

I would still have *everything* in the reality of God's presence.

And I wouldn't trade it for *anything*.

NOW I can see.

19

ALREADY IN LOVE

REAL CONTENTMENT

IT COULDN'T HAVE been a more beautiful day.

I was on our boat with my immediate family and my best friend, Rachel, and her husband, Matt.

They were visiting for the weekend.

I was in a familiar moment.

On the boat I had ridden on since I was a child.

I always sat in the same spot, on the right side of the front where I could lounge with my legs outstretched.

Right in front of the driver's seat, where I could turn my head and glance at my dad and expect a contented smile.

It was heavenly weather, 80 degrees with a slight breeze.

The sunset splitting the sky into bursts of blue, orange, pink, and streaks of vibrant, white clouds.

We were cruising slowly when I turned around and saw both of my brothers and their wives snuggling in the back so sweetly.

One of my brothers said jokingly,

"This is the love corner."

Rachel and Matt sat just a few feet to my left, snuggling in the lounge area opposite of me.

My heart started to go *there*.

To jealousy.

Discontentment.

Frustration.

A "why me" mentality.

A "this is unfair" mentality.

Painful, disappointing memories starting to rise.

But then, *I looked up.*

I caught myself and shifted.

I paid attention.

I positioned myself to see God instead.

Multiple planes were racing through the sky.

Leaving vibrant trails behind them.

Not the normal white color, but instead the trails were bursting pink-orange.

Because they were reflecting the sunset against a bright blue sky.

Everything within me became still for a sacred moment.

And *I could see.*

Not the jealousy, not the earthly desire, not the differences, not the pain from the past.

I heard God whisper,

"*You're already in love, My sweet one.*"

I felt an immediate, deep sob within my heart, causing my eyes to glisten.

I was already in the love corner.

My life was already filled with awe, wonder, and romance.

I was already fully living.

I was the furthest thing from alone.

No matter what the world tried to scream at me.

I feel no condemnation for desiring a spouse.

There is nothing wrong with that.

But God continues to remind me that if I am ever obsessed with anything besides Him, I will be missing out.

I will be disappointed no matter what with anything outside of Him.

He reminds me that there are thousands of married people who feel discontent, frustrated, and completely alone.

Because root contentment, satisfaction, and an abundant life have literally nothing to do with human relationships, whatever the form.

Contentment has everything to do with knowing and accepting the truth of eternal reality and living this temporary time in God's presence.

While I am in this earthly body, I will aim to live abundantly *now*.

I will continue to fight against the lie that we have to reach certain milestones to "fully live" or "start our lives" or to be a "real adult."

I will strive to never "live temporary" because I am waiting for some certain thing to happen.

This is a ploy of Satan that could literally destroy a person's entire life.

If I am not content now, Satan will continue to tempt me to be obsessed with attaining the next "greatest thing" whether that be a godly marriage, children, a certain job, a certain body type, a house, serving others... it will never satisfy.

I have to fully grasp and remind myself that He is my satisfaction.

Not just a comforting belief, but literal, tangible, magical, everyday life experience.

Which is only possible if I diligently commit myself to Him and make Him my number one priority.

None of this is easy.

We are promised hardship.

We are told that the world will hate us.

I will struggle, I will experience more pain, and it will be hard.

But I will always come back to my love corner.

My prayer is that my life path will look like those plane contrails I saw in the sky that evening on the boat.

A path bursting with glorious, vibrant, captivating colors reflecting the sun.

A path that looks different than all the others that tend to start blending together.

Because a life lived with real faith looks different.

A life only possible if I consistently draw back to my love corner with God.

A life only possible if I realize that I'm already in love.

NOW I can see.

> *Don't copy the behavior and customs of this world,* **but let God transform you into a new person by changing the way you think.** *Then you will learn to know God's will for you, which is good and pleasing and perfect.* (Romans 12:2, NLT, emphasis added)

I HAVE SOMEONE I WANT YOU TO MEET

REAL TRUST

I COULD FEEL a pang of jealousy, longing, and agony in my heart.

Nothing that anyone could see on the outside.

I was running around the yard with a bunch of kids playing tag.

I was twenty-five.

I was at my cousin's high school graduation party.

Every relative around my age came with their spouse and some with their kids.

And there I was chasing my niece around and dancing with kids I didn't know.

My aunt introduced me to her friend who was some of the kids' mother.

My mom told me later that this woman had said something along the lines of,

"I can see how much your daughter loves and knows Jesus through her smile."

This was encouraging.

This is all I could ever really want.

But I still longed.

～

The day before this, I had made a meal for a couple at my church who had a newborn baby.

I loved meeting and holding her and listening to my friend/new mama talk about how the birth process went.

I was reminded in this moment how we can hold such genuine contradictions at once.

I was so authentically happy for her, but jealous at the same time.

My vision was blurry as I pulled out of their driveway, eyes watering, alone in my car going home to no one.

～

After the graduation party, my immediate family and I went to my brother's house.

They asked me about a guy I had mentioned a few weeks prior who had expressed interest in me.

I didn't even know how to express myself or how to begin to explain.

I summarized as best as I could.

I knew God had given me a few specific messages a few months prior.

As time went on, my humanity kicked in and I struggled with some doubt, but I knew in my spirit that the words and warnings were real.

The first one was that God was going to start "revealing secrets" to me about my future spouse.

The second was a warning: to "beware of the counterfeit."

To remember to intentionally remain in step with the Spirit and exercise intentional discernment when it came to any men approaching me with interest.

I was hesitant to even consider these words because I was trying so hard not to idolize nor expect marriage. I had really learned what contentment meant and didn't want to backslide.

But through time with God, I realized it was okay to start thinking about it.

I knew the desire for marriage was in my heart from Him, but I wanted to make sure I was acting on His timing and not on mine.

A few weeks after receiving these messages, I was sitting on the porch at our family's lake cottage spending time with the Lord.

I was writing in my journal and I started thinking about something my mom had asked me.

She asked if I had ever asked God about my future spouse and what he is like.

I told her that I hadn't really asked, at least not super intentionally.

I spontaneously asked God and wrote down the question,

"Oh Lord, what will he be like?"

There are no words in any human language that I could use to explain this moment, but God's gentle, clear words came pouring into my spirit and reflected themselves on the page as I wrote at what felt like lightning speed.

They were not details about what he looks like or what he does for a living.

They were details about our life together.

Things like *"Your home will be a sanctuary,"*

"People will come to know Me because of your wedding,"

And *"He will want to be with Me before he is with you."*

All things that are deeply important to me.

The details became super specific.

Including the first name of my husband and the name of a future son.

Whether symbolic or literal, I am not sure.

But I will find out when God reveals him to me.

It's so interesting to think back to that moment now.

I was so chill… thankful… content… grateful.

It was information I wouldn't have been mature enough to receive a few years prior.

I could take the information with gladness and contentment.

Knowing God's timing was perfect and that I didn't *need* marriage.

Things started to become more real when several godly guys reached out to me in the days following receiving these words from God about my husband.

When I asked God what I should do concerning one of them, I felt strongly that I was supposed to hang out with him, but not to pursue anything romantically.

Um, what?

This was not how the world worked or what I was told to do by the culture around me.

Wouldn't this be leading him on?

The more I weighed it, the more right it felt.

My culture would have said to just text him and tell him I wasn't interested.

I wanted to honor him and sending a written message didn't feel right.

I wanted him to feel seen.

We had a video call because he lived a few hours away and I told him that I felt God said no to pursue anything, but that I would be willing to still get coffee or something.

I was straight up and really proud of myself–even if my explanation felt like a mess.

It was super uncomfortable.

But I realized why it was easier now to be so real with him than it had been for me in situations like this in the past.

I had nothing to lose, nothing to fear, nothing to prove, and nothing to hide.

Because I knew and loved who I was and felt no need to gain his affection or impress him in any way.

We ended up getting together the following weekend and talked for over six hours.

A lot of the conversation was about God.

We were clearly very different and had different views spiritually.

But we had a good time and challenged each other in a few areas.

We had a follow up video call and I knew I needed to make sure I communicated clearly with him.

I shared with him the Scripture I knew God was reminding me of over and over from Song of Solomon 8:4:

> *I adjure you, O daughters of Jerusalem, that you not stir up or awake love until it pleases.* (ESV)

Or as some versions say, "*...until the time is right.*"

I don't really know what the purpose of the whole thing with this guy was.

Perhaps the conversations about God were to spur each other on in different ways.

But ultimately, I know I listened to God and followed through, regardless of what people around me might have thought.

The other guy was a different story.

Because I was deeply interested for a period of time.

I saw the beauty of his spirit the very first time I saw him.

The more I got to know him, the more attracted I became.

He also started to become an incredible friend who I felt super known by and comfortable with.

This situation was much trickier, challenging, and painful for me.

I asked God what I was supposed to do.

And in time I knew the answer very clearly.

I was supposed to tell this guy what God told me about my future husband.

I was honestly a little heartbroken.

I didn't want to tell him.

Because I knew as soon as I told him, he would believe it, too, and respect it with everything he was.

And he would step back.

But I wanted him to pursue me…

A huge part of me wanted him to be *him*.

But a key piece God said to me was that *I will know.*

And whether my future spouse was this guy or not, I didn't know at that moment.

And when God tells me something, I know every single piece of it will be true.

On a walk with this man, I told him every detail of what God had communicated to me.

It was so easy and natural because of who this guy is.

And painful.

His response blew me away.

His heart overwhelmed me.

We both agreed the very best way we could both honor one another was to set boundaries, push one another to God in every way possible, and individually listen to God and pursue Him with a vengeance.

Something he said a few days later annoyed me in the moment, but rang true in my heart and still does today.

After an evening of worshiping the Lord together, I had said something along the lines of,

"How can it get better than that?"

He responded with a simple,

"That's the thing, it can."

He said this in view of God's greater plan for our lives.

Just because something looks like an awesome opportunity, God might have something even greater planned.

It's simpler than the world makes it out to be...

But it doesn't make it easy.

This man has become one of my best guy friends whom I cherish.

I am so grateful we set boundaries and realized we needed to be careful to not act on our emotions or earthly desires.

I finished my all-over-the-place explanation to my family.

I can remember one of my brothers asking,

"So you're really not going to date this guy?"

And I simply said no.

I could see his confusion.

And I understood.

I felt like crying, but I held it in.

Sometimes our obedience to God looks silly from other people's point of view.

Several years before these specific words above about my husband, God gave me a beautiful vision.

It was a gift from God shortly after a hard breakup.

The vision was of me in my "secret place" with God.

We were simply together delighting in each other–dancing and having fun.

Suddenly, I heard a rustling in the bushes.

Which was weird because no one came into my secret place except for me and God.

I ran behind God.

Just like a shy child hides behind the leg of a parent.

I peeked out to see what was happening.

I heard God speak clearly.

So gentle and sweet, yet strong.

"Fayth, I have someone I want you to meet."

A man walked into my secret place.

I couldn't see what he looked like. I only knew that God had brought this man into my secret place and that this was *only something God could do.*

From that day on, I knew that when God wants me to marry someone, He will cleary say to me,

"Fayth, I have someone I want you to meet."

And I will know.

A random night following that conversation with my family, I knew God told me it was time.

I could start praying for *him*.

This felt weird.

I was afraid.

For years, I had tried to not idolize marriage, and encouraged people not to see it as the end goal of life.

For me for a certain period of time, it felt that praying for a spouse would only fan the flame of marriage idolization.

It would cause me to expect marriage, rather than being open to singleness and whatever God had planned for my life.

It's so common to hear things such as *"you'll understand when you're married"* and *"wait until you have kids."*

I realized as an adult that these words are from culture, not from God.

These types of words can be destructive as they make singleness look as if it is a problem to be solved.

These words tell children that they WILL get married, and if they don't, something might be wrong with them.

This is a lie and probably has devastated so many lives because people believe they have to get married to be content, happy, and purposeful–when this is not what God's Word says at all.

I only wanted to pray for my spouse if God told me to.

If His plan for my life included marriage.

And after several years, He did.

The moment felt sacred as I walked into my room, kneeled on the rug, prayed, and sang over this man as I cried.

⌇

Sometimes I feel really alone.

There are times when I feel like no one around me is listening to God.

I know that this is not true, but sometimes I look around and it feels like people just control their own lives and don't ask God for their next steps.

I know I sometimes might look foolish or naive to other people.

Why would you tell a guy you're not interested but still go out with him?

Why would you not date an insanely godly man whom you adore who's also interested?

Why would you believe that God spoke to you about someone you possibly don't know yet?

Because real faith looks different.

A faith that trusts God's voice before anything else.

⌇

We need to remember and reflect on what God asked of His servants in the Bible times.

Noah was insane.

People probably thought he was an absolute idiot.

He spent years of his life and resources building a giant–and I mean GIANT–boat.

Because God told Noah He was going to flood the earth and kill everyone except for him, his family, and each animal kind.

It didn't even really rain where Noah was.

Yet, he followed through.

Regardless of the mockery he must have received from his neighbors (and potentially his own family) who probably thought he was crazy.

Neighbors who eventually drowned…

~

Ruth was a woman who was widowed at a young age.

In her culture, her streamlined focus should have been on getting married for her own survival and well-being.

But she sacrificed her life to travel to a foreign land to take care of her heartbroken mother-in-law who was also a widow.

We have to grasp that she was not simply doing a favor, she was sacrificing her very life.

In this foreign land, she gleaned in a field which just so happened to be owned by a man named Boaz who was a relative of her mother-in-law's husband.

Some say coincidence, I say God.

Long story short, Boaz honored and took care of Ruth and her mother-in-law.

And ultimately married Ruth.

Their son, Obed, would become the father of Jesse, who would become the father of King David.

> If we say we love God, we must listen to Him, have faith in what He speaks to us, and follow through–even if we look like a nutcase.

Ruth's obedience led to her birthing a baby included in the genealogy of Jesus Christ.

God's faithful servant, Abraham, had prayed for a son for years.

When he finally had this beloved son, Isaac, God told Abraham to kill his son and sacrifice him as a burnt offering.

Are you kidding me?

This literally makes no logical sense.

In fact, it's horrible.

Abraham had to have heard God wrong, right?

There is no way God would tell him to do this.

But He did.

And Abraham *painfully obeyed*.

To the point of traveling for days to get to the place God told him to sacrifice his son!

Can you imagine?

Abraham gave Isaac wood to carry while he carried the fire and the knife as they walked the final distance to the place where his son would be sacrificed.

Isaac asked his father where the lamb was for the offering.

Imagine the agony in Abraham's heart!

He told Isaac that God would provide the lamb.

When Abraham raised the knife, an angel of the Lord called from heaven to stop him.

> *Do not lay your hand on the boy or do anything to him, for now I know that you fear God, seeing you have not withheld your son, your only son, from me.* (Genesis 22:12, ESV)

Why did God test Abraham in such an extreme way?

This I don't know.

But as a result of Abraham's faith, God promised that through his descendants the nations would be blessed *because of his obedience.*

Imagine that trip home and explaining to your wife that you almost killed your son…

If Noah, Ruth, or Abraham trusted what their "culture" said to them or other people's opinions… you can imagine the alternate endings.

What pleases God is faith, reliance, and trust in Him.

What pleases God is obedience.

Second John 1:6 reads,

> And this is love, that we walk according to his commandments...
> (ESV)

If we say we love God, we must listen to Him, have faith in what He speaks to us, and follow through–even if we look like a nutcase.

A dear friend once said to me,

"God loves to show off the ones He loves."

He certainly did this with Noah, Ruth, and Abraham.

I want to walk in their footsteps.

Until God reveals my husband to me, I won't be waiting.

I will be living.

I will still be joyfully running across the yard with the kids playing tag.

I can trust God because I know Him.

And ultimately, I know in my heart I already have *everything* in the reality of His presence.

NOW I can see.

*In those days Mary arose and went with haste into the hill country, to a town in Judah, and she entered the house of Zechariah and greeted Elizabeth. And when Elizabeth heard the greeting of Mary, the baby leaped in her womb. And Elizabeth was filled with the Holy Spirit, and she exclaimed with a loud cry, "Blessed are you among women, and blessed is the fruit of your womb! And why is this granted to me that the mother of my Lord should come to me? For behold, when the sound of your greeting came to my ears, the baby in my womb leaped for joy. And **blessed is she who believed that there would be a fulfillment of what was spoken to her from the Lord.**"* (Luke 1:39-45, ESV, emphasis added)

IT WAS THE DAY AFTER CHRISTMAS

AFTERWORD

I WAS AT my parent's house.

I was in their bedroom grabbing something when I heard in my spirit,

"Come to the window."

I looked out to see a plane slicing through the bright blue sky leaving a vivid white trail.

I went to the kitchen where my family was chatting and noticed through the back window over their heads another plane threading the sky like a needle with pink thread.

I quickly turned and went to the front of the house and out the front door.

No shoes or jacket in the freezing cold–I didn't care.

The sun was sinking into the earth.

Radiant pinks and oranges burst against the blue.

Plane after plane after plane surrounded the sunset.

Each leaving pink-orange trails everywhere I looked.

I breathed in the fresh, winter air.

Suddenly, a plane appeared directly above me that was lower to the ground.

Leaving a huge trail reflecting the color of the sunset.

The plane looked like it was going so slow from my perspective, but I knew in reality it was flying at hundreds of miles per hour.

It reminded me of earthly life.

Sometimes it might look or feel slow, when in reality we are gone in a flash in comparison to eternity.

I sang a whispered song into the crisp air, a favorite from Capital City Music.[33]

With my face directly upward as I watched the plane make its way across the expanse above me.

Now I can see Your love is better
Than all the others that I've seen
I'm breathing deep all of Your goodness
And Your loving-kindness to me

NOW I can see...

I am not saying this because I am in need, for I have learned to be content whatever the circumstances. I know what it is to be in need, and I know what it is to have plenty. **I have learned the secret of being content in any and every situation**, *whether well fed or hungry, whether living in plenty or in want. I can do all this through him who gives me strength.* (Philippians 4:11-13, NIV, emphasis added)

WITH EVERYTHING I AM, THANK YOU
ACKNOWLEDGEMENTS

To **Jed (HeeLak) Lee**—for your unwavering eternal outlook.

To **Bethany Hastings**–for your life-giving prophecy and faith.

To **Shelbi Strube**–for filling me with godly confidence.

To **Isaac Dees**—for your belief in me.

To **Anna Foster**–for your intentional, joyful encouragement.

To **Kaitlyn Bookmyer**—for your joy and faith in my writing.

To **Rebekah Schwulst, Rachel German**, and **Amy Frederickson**–for being my biggest fans.

To **Savannah Dize**—for always reminding me of who I am.

To **Rachel Matyszczak**—for holding me up in my pain and for being my constant source of truth.

To **my grandma, Diana Horzelski**—for loving me fiercely.

To **my grampy, Bernard Horzelski**—for seeing me the way God does.

To **my mom, Deb Glock**—for every sacrifice you've made for me, your constant listening heart, and your unwavering love.

To **my dad, Jeff Glock**—for empowering me to greater things, providing for me, and tangibly loving and supporting me in everything I do.

To all my additional friends and family who played a role in this journey, I am eternally grateful for you.

*An extra special thanks to **Rachel M.** and my **dad**, my beloved editors.*

TO THE WRITERS WHO HAVE GONE BEFORE ME

To Oboitshepo Tladi–for your obedient, loving, *real* voice.

To Steffany Gretzinger–for your lyrics that bring me closer to God's heart.

To Ann Voskamp–for teaching me how to intentionally live in real gratitude.

To Corrie and Betsie ten Boom–for teaching me how to worship, experience, and honor God amidst horrific suffering.

To C.S. Lewis–for sharing your imagination and heart with me.

To Eric Gilmour–for teaching me how to practically enter the presence of God and experience His presence.

Because you wrote the world was changed and will continue to change. Thank you for having the courage and obedience to write your heart for the world to see. I can only hope that my writing will bring someone closer to God as your writing has done for me and he or she might say...

"Because she wrote."

MEET THE AUTHOR

FAYTH GLOCK is a daughter, sister, aunt, friend, writer, poet, and spoken word artist. She currently works as a content strategist in web development and enjoys serving through her personal writing platform, *Covenant Poetry*. Fayth is grounded in the Midwest but has a heart for traveling to unknown places. Her mission on this earth is to know and love God, and to inspire others to do the same.

DISCOVER MORE OF FAYTH'S WRITING AT: **COVENANTPOETRY.COM**

ENDNOTES

EPIGRAPH

1. Lewis, C. S. (2017). *The Four Loves.* San Francisco: HarperOne.

ENTERING IN

2. Gilmour, E. (n.d.). *School of His Presence.* Retrieved December 30, 2020, from https://www.sonship-international.org/school-of-his-presence

3. Gilmour, E. (n.d.).*INSTRUMENTAL WORSHIP* [Eric Gilmour]. Youtube. Retrieved December 30, 2020, from https://www.youtube.com/c/EricGilmour/playlists

4. Gilmour, E. W. (2018). *The School of His Presence.* CreateSpace Independent Publishing Platform.

5. Voskamp, A. (2012). *One Thousand Gifts Devotional: Reflections on Finding Everyday Graces.* Zondervan.

6. Ibid.

THE SECRET PLACE

7. Bethel Music (2018, April 2). *All That Lives Forever* (Official Lyric Video) - Steffany Gretzinger | BLACKOUT [Video]. YouTube. https://www.youtube.com/watch?v=uVbZ05ZWM3E

ANYWAYS, ALWAYS

8. Voskamp, A. (2017, December 10). *...so on a quiet Sunday, the Lord's day, the second Sunday in Advent...I will slow & I will quiet & I will ponder His coming.* [Image attached] [Status update]. Facebook. https://www.facebook.com/324577877554393/photos/ a.369461463066034/1813816328630533/?type=3

9. Voskamp, A. (2012). *One Thousand Gifts Devotional: Reflections on Finding Everyday Graces.* Zondervan. (emphasis added)

10. Ten Boom, C. (2006). *The Hiding Place (35th Anniversary ed.).* Chosen Books.

SO THIS IS LOVE

11. Bethel Music (2014, October 3). *Out of Hiding* (Official Lyric Video) - Steffany Gretzinger & Amanda Cook | *The Undoing* [Video]. YouTube. https://youtu.be/XFkDqQtfs0w (emphasis added)

SO THIS IS WHAT IT MEANS

12. Ibid.

FOREVER I DO

13. Ruelle. (2016, March 11). *RUELLE - I Get To Love You* (Official Music Video) [Video]. YouTube. https://youtu.be/ m1mkYWkoXyo

14. Elvis Presley. (2013, April 23). Elvis Presley - *Can't Help Falling In Love* (Audio) [Video]. YouTube. https://youtu.be/vGJTaP6anOU

15. Ben Rector. (2018, August 9). *When I'm With You* [Video]. YouTube. https://youtu.be/1dxc9YPnBjU

16. Lea Michele. (2017, April 3). *Lea Michele - Run to You* (Audio) [Video]. YouTube. https://youtu.be/D2C96iZHObk

17. *NSYNC. (2009, October 25). *NSYNC - This I Promise You* (Official Music Video) [Video]. YouTube. https://youtu.be/ 6thmPrTxBtI

18. Ruelle Music. [@ruellemusic]. (2016, April 22). The story behind *"I Get To Love You"*... [Tweet]. Twitter. https://twitter.com/ ruellemusic/status/723559327294873600

STOP ACTING LIKE GROWN UPS

19. Cosper, M. (2017). *Recapturing the Wonder: Transcendent Faith in a Disenchanted World.* Downers Grove, IL: IVP Books, an imprint of InterVarsity Press.

20. Lewis, C. S. (2004). *Chronicles of Narnia* (Illustrated ed.). HarperCollins.

21. Adamson, A. (Director), Adamson, A., Johnson, M., & Steuer, P. (Producers), & Adamson, A., Peacock, A., Markus, C., McFeely, S., & Neeson, L. (Writers). (2008). *The Chronicles of Narnia, Prince Caspian* [Motion Picture]. United States: Walt Disney Studios Motion Pictures.

22. *Wonder.* (n.d.). Retrieved January 02, 2021, from https:// www.merriam-webster.com/dictionary/wonder

23. Bethel Music. (2014, May 7). *Wonder* (Spontaneous) - Amanda Cook | *You Make Me Brave* [Video]. YouTube. https://youtu.be/ 3F7lxt5fTeo

WHAT DID YOU DO TODAY?

24. Johnson, B. (2017, May 12). *Busyness is artificial significance* [Status update]. Facebook. https://www.facebook.com/ BillJohnsonMinistries/posts/busyness-is-artificial-significance/ 10154978538573387/

I FEEL IT EVERYDAY

25. Laney Rene. (2019, October 31). *"NO FEAR"* BY LANEY RENE [Video]. YouTube. https://youtu.be/j3ga2bUf-cc (emphasis added)

26. *Wisdom.* (n.d.). Retrieved January 02, 2021, from https:// www.merriam-webster.com/dictionary/wisdom

OWN YOUR BELOVEDNESS

27. Sarah Kroger. (2020, December 16). *Belovedness - Sarah Kroger* (Live Release Show) [Video]. YouTube. https://youtu.be/QlcoEC-hNfg

28. Chbosky, S. (Director), & Malkovich, J., Smith, R., & Halfon, L. (Producers). (2012). *The Perks of Being a Wallflower* [Motion Picture]. United States: Summit Entertainment.

29. Warren, R. (2002). *The Purpose Driven Life: What on Earth Am I Here For?* (1st ed.). Zondervan.

FOR WHAT?

30. Oboitshepo Tladi. (.n.d.). *Home* [YouTube channel] Retrieved January 2, 2021, from https://www.youtube.com/channel/UCkZ-ug9OSIXeVYKH1YgSG_w

31. Praytell. (2018, February 2). *Praytell | I'd Pick You* [Video]. https://youtu.be/tK550jtYb68

I WILL DANCE WEIRD, NOW

32. Voskamp, A. (2012). *One Thousand Gifts Devotional: Reflections on Finding Everyday Graces.* Zondervan.

IT WAS THE DAY AFTER CHRISTMAS

33. Capital City Music. (2018, January 23). *Lean Back* (+Spontaneous) | Capital City Music | Live from Washington, DC | *Kingdom Come Album* [Video]. YouTube. https://www.youtube.com/watch?v=qHQOcUizZuQ

Made in the USA
Monee, IL
01 August 2023

40197877R00109